Mastering QuickBooks Online

The Step-By-Step Guide to Stress-Free Bookkeeping for Freelancers and Small Business Owners

Zachary Foster

Table of Contents

Introduction

In the ever-evolving world of business, the need for efficient, reliable, and user-friendly financial management tools has never been greater. As businesses grow and adapt to the changing economic landscape, so too must the tools they rely on to manage their finances. Enter QuickBooks Online (QBO) - a cloud-based accounting solution designed to meet the unique needs of businesses of all sizes.

This book is your comprehensive guide to mastering this powerful accounting software. Whether you're a seasoned business owner looking to switch from another platform, a budding entrepreneur setting up your financials for the first time, or an accountant aiming to sharpen your QBO skills, this book has something for everyone.

The chapters are meticulously structured to provide a step-by-step journey through every facet of QBO. From the basics of setting up your account to the intricacies of financial reporting and analysis, each chapter delves deep into its topic, ensuring you gain a thorough understanding of its features and functionalities.

Chapter 1 sets the stage, introducing you to the world of QuickBooks Online, its myriad benefits, and the various subscription plans available. As you progress, you'll learn to navigate the user-friendly interface of QBO, set up your company profile, manage financial accounts, and delve into the nuances of customer, vendor, and inventory management.

But this book is not just about the *how-to*. It's about understanding the *why* behind each feature. Why is it essential to reconcile your bank accounts? Why is understanding the Chart of Accounts crucial for your business's financial health? Why are closing periods vital for accurate financial reporting? By the end of this guide, you won't just know how to use QuickBooks Online; you'll understand the significance of each feature and its impact on your business operations.

Moreover, as businesses are not just about numbers and ledgers, this book also covers the human side of things - payroll and employee management. Learn how to set up payroll, manage employee information, handle payroll taxes, and more.

In the later chapters, we delve into the more advanced features of QBO, including third-party integrations, mastering journal entries, and leveraging QBO's advanced features. And for when things don't go as planned, Chapter 14 offers invaluable troubleshooting advice and time-saving tips to ensure you get the most out of your QBO experience.

QuickBooks Online is more than just a guide; it's a companion. A companion that will walk with you as you embark on your journey through the world of online accounting, ensuring that no question goes unanswered and no feature is unexplored.

So, whether you're a novice just starting out or a seasoned pro looking to brush up on your skills, this book is your roadmap to mastering QuickBooks Online. Let's embark on this journey together and unlock the full potential of your business's financial management. Welcome to QuickBooks Online.

Chapter 1

Introduction to QuickBooks Online

As the world of business continues to evolve and adapt to technological advancements, efficient and reliable financial management becomes paramount for the success of any organization. In today's digital era, businesses are constantly seeking innovative methods to refine their accounting procedures, enhance accuracy, and get an immediate overview of their financial situation. Developed by Intuit, QuickBooks Online is a cloud-based accounting solution that stands out as a leader, providing companies with the essential tools to excel in the financial sector

Overview of QuickBooks Online

In the dynamic and fast-paced world of business, the need for efficient and reliable accounting software has never been greater. QuickBooks Online (QBO), developed by Intuit, has emerged as a leading cloud-based accounting solution, offering a comprehensive suite of financial management tools tailored to meet the diverse needs of businesses ranging from small startups to large enterprises.

At its core, QuickBooks Online is designed to simplify the often complex and time-consuming tasks associated with financial management. As a cloud-based platform, it eschews the traditional desktop software model, enabling users to access their financial data and perform critical accounting functions from any internet-enabled device, whether it be a computer, tablet, or smartphone. This level of accessibility ensures that business owners and finance professionals are not tethered to a specific location, liberating them from managing their finances on the go.

One of the standout features of QuickBooks Online is its user-friendly interface. Intuit has dedicated considerable resources to develop an intuitive interface that gives users a succinct and clear snapshot of their financial standing. Key financial metrics, such as bank account balances, outstanding invoices, and expense reports, are presented in a visually appealing manner, enabling even those without extensive accounting knowledge to grasp their financial health at a glance. This simplicity empowers business owners to make informed decisions quickly and efficiently.

Furthermore, QuickBooks Online offers a vast array of features that go beyond basic accounting tasks. The software's integration capabilities allow for seamless connectivity with numerous third-party applications, such as payment processors, e-commerce platforms, and customer relationship management (CRM) software. This integration creates a unified ecosystem that optimizes productivity by streamlining processes and minimizing the need for manual data entry. As a result, businesses can leverage the power of multiple tools, working together harmoniously, to create a more holistic approach to financial management.

With the growing concern about data security in the digital age, QuickBooks Online prioritizes safeguarding sensitive financial information. Intuit employs state-of-the-art encryption and security protocols to protect user data from unauthorized access and cyber threats. Additionally, the cloud-based nature of the software ensures that data is regularly and automatically backed up, alleviating the fear of losing critical financial records due to hardware malfunctions or system crashes.

For businesses seeking real-time financial insights, QuickBooks Online stands as an indispensable ally. The software provides up-to-the-minute updates and generates reports that enable users to monitor cash flow, track expenses, and review profitability at any moment. This level of agility empowers decision-makers to respond promptly to changing market dynamics and make informed strategic choices.

Another significant advantage of using QuickBooks Online is the time-saving automation it brings to accounting processes. The software automates various tasks, such as bank reconciliations, invoice generation, and expense tracking. This automated process doesn't just lower the chances of mistakes made by humans; it also conserves precious time for finance team. Freed from the burden of manual data entry and repetitive tasks, finance professionals can focus on more value-added activities, such as financial analysis and business planning, contributing to the overall growth and success of the organization.

QuickBooks Online's adaptability is another strength that attracts businesses of all sizes. As a company grows, its financial management needs also evolve. It is designed to accommodate these changes, providing the scalability required to support businesses from their humble beginnings to their successful ventures. The software allows users to customize reports, charts of accounts, and templates to suit their specific requirements, tailoring the platform to their unique financial ecosystem.

Collaboration and teamwork are essential components of any successful business. QuickBooks Online caters to this need by enabling multiple users to collaborate simultaneously on financial tasks. The software allows users to grant access to specific data and functionalities based on individual roles, ensuring that each team member has the necessary information and tools to contribute effectively. This collaborative approach fosters a sense of cohesion within the organization and promotes smoother financial workflows.

As with any software, customer support is critical for users seeking help and guidance. Intuit recognizes this importance and provides comprehensive customer support for QuickBooks Online users. Additionally, the company regularly updates the software to enhance its features, improve security, and address any reported issues. These updates are delivered automatically to users, ensuring they always have access to the latest enhancements and refinements.

Benefits of Using QuickBooks Online

In the ever-evolving landscape of business, staying ahead in the financial arena is crucial for sustained growth and success. QuickBooks Online (QBO), as a leading cloud-based accounting software, offers a myriad of benefits that empower businesses of all sizes to effectively manage their finances, make informed decisions, and optimize their overall operations. Let's delve into the various advantages that make QuickBooks Online a preferred choice among accounting solutions:

Accessibility and Mobility

QuickBooks Online's cloud-based nature is a game-changer in accessibility and mobility. Users can access their financial data and perform essential accounting tasks from any internet-connected device, be it a desktop computer, laptop, tablet, or smartphone. This level of flexibility liberates business owners and finance professionals from the constraints of a physical office, empowering them to manage their finances on the go. Whether attending meetings, traveling for business, or working remotely, users can stay connected with their financial data and take timely actions as needed.

Real-Time Financial Insights

In the fast-paced and competitive business environment, timely access to financial information is paramount. QuickBooks Online provides real-time updates and generates reports that allow users to monitor cash flow, track expenses, and review profitability at any given moment. This up-to-date visibility empowers decision-makers to make informed choices promptly, respond swiftly to market changes, and devise effective strategies for business growth.

Automation and Time-Saving

QuickBooks Online streamlines various accounting processes through automation, resulting in significant time savings for finance teams. Tasks such as bank reconciliations, invoice generation, and expense tracking are automated, reducing the need for manual data entry and minimizing the risk of errors. With these routine tasks taken care of, finance professionals can focus on more strategic activities, such as financial analysis and business planning, adding greater value to the organization.

Data Security and Backups

Ensuring the security of financial data is a top priority for any business. QuickBooks Online employs robust security measures, including advanced encryption and authentication protocols, to safeguard sensitive financial information from unauthorized access and potential cyber threats. Additionally, as a cloud-based platform, the software automatically backs up data on a regular basis, protecting against data loss due to hardware failures or other unforeseen events. This reassurance of data security provides peace of mind to business owners, allowing them to concentrate on their core operations.

Scalability and Customization

Businesses evolve and grow over time, and their financial management needs change accordingly. QuickBooks Online is designed with scalability in mind, catering to businesses at various stages of growth. As a business grows, QuickBooks Online is capable of handling the escalating intricacy of its financial activities. Moreover, the software allows users to customize reports, charts of accounts, and templates to suit their specific requirements, tailoring the platform to fit their unique financial ecosystem.

Cost-Effectiveness

QuickBooks Online offers a cost-effective solution compared to traditional on-premises accounting software. With no upfront investment in hardware and infrastructure, businesses can save on installation and maintenance costs. The subscription-based model of QuickBooks Online ensures that users receive regular updates and customer support without incurring additional charges. Additionally, the time saved through automation translates to increased productivity and cost efficiency for the organization.

Collaboration and User Management

In today's collaborative work environment, effective teamwork is essential for success. QuickBooks Online enables multiple users to access the platform simultaneously, facilitating collaboration among team members. Depending on their roles and responsibilities, users can be granted specific permissions to access relevant financial data and functionalities. This feature ensures that each team member can contribute effectively to financial tasks, leading to streamlined workflows and improved productivity.

Regular Updates and Support

QuickBooks Online is continuously updated to enhance its features, improve security, and address any reported issues. These updates are automatically delivered to users, ensuring that they always have access to the latest advancements and refinements. Additionally, Intuit, the developer of QuickBooks Online, provides comprehensive customer support to assist users with any queries or technical challenges they may encounter, further enhancing the user experience.

Integration with Third-Party Applications

QuickBooks Online integration capabilities expand its functionality beyond accounting. The software seamlessly integrates with numerous third-party applications, including payment processors, e-commerce platforms, CRM systems, and payroll services. This integration forms a cohesive network that simplifies business procedures and cuts down on the necessity for entering data more than once. By leveraging these integrations, businesses can optimize their workflows and achieve greater operational efficiency.

Choosing the Right Subscription Plan

Selecting the appropriate subscription plan is a crucial step in implementing QuickBooks Online (QBO) for any business. With multiple tiers of plans tailored to meet different needs, understanding the features and limitations of each option is essential to ensure that businesses get the most value out of their chosen plan. Below is an in-depth exploration of the typical subscription plans offered by QuickBooks Online, helping businesses make an informed decision.

Pro Tip: Take the Software for a Test Drive with a 30-day Free Trial

The 30-day free trial option for QuickBooks is an excellent opportunity for individuals and businesses to experience the software's robust features before committing to a purchase. During this trial period, users can explore QuickBooks' intuitive interface, streamline their financial processes, and gain a comprehensive understanding of how it can benefit their specific needs. QuickBooks offers various plans tailored to different business sizes and requirements, ensuring that you can choose the one that suits you best. To make an informed decision about which plan to eventually purchase, I recommend visiting the official pricing page at https://quickbooks.intuit.com/pricing/. There, you can review detailed information about each plan and select the one that aligns perfectly with your accounting and financial management needs.

Simple Start	Essentials	Plus	Advanced
$15/mo	**$30/mo**	**$45/mo**	**$100/mo**
Choose plan	Choose plan	Choose plan	Choose plan

Simple Start

The Simple Start plan is the entry-level offering of QuickBooks Online, designed for small businesses, freelancers, and sole proprietors with basic accounting requirements. This plan is an excellent starting point for those who need a streamlined accounting solution without the complexity of advanced features. Some key features of the Simple Start plan include:

- **Income and Expense Tracking:** Users can easily record and categorize income and expenses, providing an overview of the business's financial activities.
- **Invoice Creation and Sending:** The plan enables users to create and send professional invoices to clients, facilitating smooth payment processes.
- **Bank Reconciliation:** Users can connect their bank accounts to QBO and reconcile transactions to ensure accurate and up-to-date financial records.

While the Simple Start plan is cost-effective and ideal for micro-businesses, it has limitations compared to higher-tier plans. For instance, it supports only one user, lacks the ability to manage bills and track time, and doesn't offer advanced reporting features. As a result, businesses with more complex accounting needs or multiple users may find the Simple Start plan limiting in the long run.

Essentials

The Essentials plan is a step up from Simple Start and is aimed at small to medium-sized businesses that require more robust accounting functionalities. This plan includes all the features of the Simple Start plan and offers additional capabilities, making it suitable for businesses seeking more comprehensive financial management. Key features of the Essentials plan include:

- **Multiple User Access:** The plan allows up to three users to access and collaborate on financial data, which is advantageous for businesses with multiple team members handling accounting tasks.
- **Bill Management:** Users can manage and track bills, making it easier to stay on top of payables and manage cash flow effectively.
- **Time Tracking:** This feature enables businesses to track the time spent on projects or tasks, facilitating accurate invoicing and project management.

The Essentials plan bridges the gap between basic accounting and more advanced features, making it a preferred choice for businesses looking to expand their financial capabilities. However, businesses with more complex inventory management needs or those requiring budgeting and reporting functionalities may need to explore higher-tier plans.

Plus

The Plus plan is the most popular option among QuickBooks Online subscribers and is geared towards growing businesses with more comprehensive accounting requirements. It includes all the features of the Essentials plan and offers additional benefits, making it a well-rounded option for businesses seeking a robust accounting solution. Key features of the Plus plan include:

- **Inventory Tracking:** Users can track inventory levels, costs, and sales, providing valuable insights into the inventory management process.
- **Project Profitability Analysis:** This feature allows businesses to analyze the profitability of individual projects, helping them make data-driven decisions.
- **Budgeting and Reporting:** Users can create budgets to plan and forecast their financials while also benefiting from advanced reporting features to gain deeper insights into their performance.

The Plus plan's advanced features make it suitable for businesses that need in-depth inventory management, budgeting, and more comprehensive reporting capabilities. With support for up to five users, it fosters better collaboration within the organization.

Advanced

The Advanced plan is the top-tier offering of QuickBooks Online, catering to larger enterprises with more complex financial management needs. In addition to all the features of the Plus plan, the Advanced plan offers a range of premium benefits, making it suitable for businesses with extensive collaboration requirements and advanced reporting needs. Key features of the Advanced plan include:

- **Accelerated Invoicing:** Users can create and automate recurring invoices, streamlining the invoicing process for efficiency.
- **Enhanced User Permissions:** The plan allows more granular control over user access and permissions, ensuring data security and privacy.
- **Priority Customer Support:** Advanced plan subscribers receive priority access to customer support, expediting issue resolution and support assistance.

With support for up to 25 users, the Advanced plan is ideal for larger organizations with multiple departments and stakeholders involved in financial management. It's advanced features and user management capabilities enable seamless collaboration and efficient financial workflows.

Chapter 2

Navigating the QBO User Interface

With the most recent version of QuickBooks Online, you can easily access your regular chores like invoicing, banking, paying your employees, and more. The language and ideas used in this streamlined experience are the same ones you use to run your business.

How To Navigate Different Modules?

We'll demonstrate the functions available in each menu tab and how to modify the menu to best suit your company's requirements.

An Overview of The Menu Options

Depending on whether you are using QuickBooks in the Accountant view or Business view, your navigation menu may look different. Tasks linked to accounting and business are grouped together in the business view. An overview of the Business View menu is provided below:

The first step in completing the fundamental duties at the center of your business is to get things done. This entails tying bank accounts together, making invoices, classifying transactions, and keeping track of receipts.

Cash flow, reports, and projects are grouped together in a business overview to help you organize your finances and see your profits clearly. In QuickBooks Online, the dynamic left navigational menu cursor is used to select the Business Overview. Quick access to financial chores and tools like QuickBooks Checking and Capital is provided through banking services. Get paid and pay for your purchases and expenses. Send invoices, get time-tracking access, pay suppliers, and keep track of your earnings over time.

You can set up and manage your clients here, as well as track their payments and promote them using MailChimp. Any major e-commerce platform you use to sell and track your goods or services is accessible through commerce. In order to manage employees and contractors, track their time and benefits, and adhere to tax and regulatory regulations, you must use payroll.

You can invite your accountant to work on your books, reconcile your bank accounts, and more with the help of bookkeeping. You can file contractor 1099 forms and set up automatic tax computations with the aid of taxes. You can find additional QuickBooks products or third-party apps for anything from tracking mileage to purchasing office furniture under the apps section.

Make Your View Unique

To make your navigation menu more suited to your requirements, you can edit it to highlight the pages you visit most frequently or conceal ones you don't. Don't worry if you can't see these options just yet; we will gradually make them available to all of our clients. Options for QuickBooks Online Business View's left menu customization and bookmarking are animated.

Make a page bookmark
- Select *Edit* next to Bookmarks.
- Choose which pages should be listed under Bookmarks.
- Select rearrange Screen Shot 2022-07-25 at 4.49.52 PM.png and drag the bookmarks into the new position to reorder them.
- Select *Save.*

Taking away a bookmark
- To access more options, hover your cursor over one of your bookmarked pages.
- Decide to remove the bookmark.

Show or hide a page
- Click *Edit Menu* next to Menu.
- You can select or deselect the pages you need.
- Select Reorder and drag the items to the new position on your menu to change the order.
- Select *Save.*

Understanding the Main Dashboard

Every company uses a few key indicators to track performance. This data is used to calculate key performance indicators, and it frequently decides whether firms or organizations succeed or fail. Your critical performance indicators can be displayed simply and effectively using the dashboard in QuickBooks Online. Having said that, there are instances when signs can only be understood when placed in the proper context with additional data, such as comparisons to earlier months, years, or budgets. Without context, a statistic may appear fine but be underwhelming when compared to a previous time. To provide more context and meaning, this necessitates the use of external technologies.

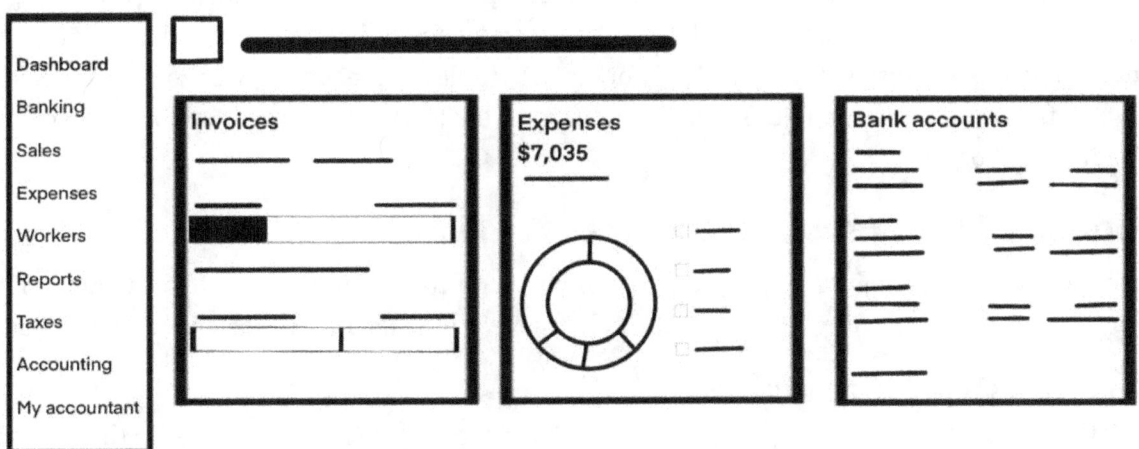

This section will demonstrate how to use the QuickBooks Online dashboard, how to manage it, and how to use third-party applications to get more sophisticated data. You may use both the built-in dashboard and a more configurable one to make informed decisions that will improve your bottom line, whether you want to expand profit margins or make a business investment.

Basics of The QuickBooks Online Dashboard

The dashboard for QuickBooks offers a look into the overall picture of your company's finances. Given the importance of tracking key performance indicators, the dashboard's built-in features provide numerous options for correctly displaying and reviewing KPIs.

The dashboard displays information in various ways and presents indicators that are most likely to have an impact on your organization. QuickBooks bar graphs are a great choice for data display for some people, such as accountants, who believe that numbers tell the story. Others who are more visually oriented might find the integrated graphical representations more suitable.

Dashboard for QuickBooks

QuickBooks gives you the ability to see, monitor, and report on important financial performance indicators; however, all representations are read-only, so you cannot change the filters or time ranges.

How to enhance the dashboard in QuickBooks

What happens, though, if you wish to draw more insightful conclusions from the data represented in QuickBooks' charts and graphs? Additionally, what if your processes and workflows require you to import or export data more frequently? The good news is that you can create a configurable dashboard outside of QuickBooks thanks to QuickBooks's ability to interact with third-party solutions. Many technologies let you export data to particular locations and see data analytics more frequently and according to predetermined schedules. For instance, Coupler.io lets you export data even once every 15 minutes to your preferred location. You can interact with this data and create countless chart types for each use case, depending on the task at hand.

Just get started

A 14-day free trial of the Coupler.io platform is available. The benefit of this platform for data integration is that you can also export your QuickBooks data into a spreadsheet and combine it with imports from other applications (such as Pipedrive, Harvest, HubSpot, and Airtable). Then, using Excel or Google Sheets, or a data visualization tool (such as Microsoft Power BI or Google Data Studio), you can construct a fully customizable dashboard.

Explanation of QuickBooks Dashboard Analytics

The QuickBooks dashboard gives you a summary of your company's operations. It provides a number of measures that make it easier for you to track the effectiveness of your operations and analyze your data.

Examples of QuickBooks dashboards

Go to your QuickBooks homepage to see your dashboard. There are two primary tabs on the dashboard:

- Gets things done

- Business overview

The second tab is for getting things done.

Under the *Get Things Done* tab, you will find three types of services: banking, explore more (assisting with QuickBooks setup), and shortcuts. You may navigate your account, personalize your invoice template, and configure you tax details according to the setup guide's directions as you set up your company's operations. With the use of shortcuts, you may use QuickBooks' features more quickly and spend less time performing routine operations. Examples of these jobs include adding a supplier, a cost, a bill, a new client, and more. The balance of the current account that is linked to QuickBooks Online is displayed in the bank accounts menu.

Tab 3 of the *Business Overview* window

It provides a comprehensive summary of your company's operations, covering sales, profit and loss, bank accounts, income and expenses. This tab is your go-to tool for tracking your company's profitability.

Within this tab, you'll find four date pickers that allow you to adjust the timescale of the bars and graphs. You can zoom in on specific time periods, ranging from the previous 30 days to the past year, by selecting your choice from the drop-down menu in the top right corner. On the right side of your dashboard, you can view information related to the account types you've set up, and you can click the 'pencil' icon to make updates. If you want to link your accounts to specific banks, simply scroll to the bottom of the list.

However, it's important to note that QuickBooks doesn't offer the option to create custom date ranges with specific start and end dates. Instead, it provides predefined date ranges to adjust the data displayed in the bars and graphs.

For more advanced data analysis, such as mapping client locations, identifying the most profitable products, or comparing revenue and expenses over custom time periods, you'll need to create a separate dashboard outside of QuickBooks. This will allow you to perform calculations and explore specific metrics before presenting your data.

How Do I Personalize My QuickBooks Online Dashboard?

The QuickBooks Online dashboard presents an advanced way to automate bookkeeping by gathering all your data in one place. Regardless of the nature and scale of your organization, some automatic functions might not be adequate for your requirements. Each business has its own set of particular objectives and requirements, which call for specialized knowledge. Fortunately, the technology enables customization of the QuickBooks Online interface to meet your specific requirements, instead of just offering a generic, one-size-fits-all solution. Some features can be changed, but not all of them.

You can organize bank accounts and linked credit card details for easy retrieval by adjusting the icons up or down based on your usage frequency. Additionally, you have the option to insert custom fields into QuickBooks to record information that the platform does not originally provide for These fields can be added to purchase orders, invoices, sales receipts, refund receipts, and other documents. You might, for example, implement a specialized field to log the salesperson in charge of a transaction and then utilize a report to assess their total sales contributions. In the end, you have the option to select how information is displayed in bars and graphs, for a broader or more detailed analysis of your financial situation. Thirty days, last month, last quarter, and last fiscal year are among the alternatives on the list.

A Different Approach to Building a Dashboard in QuickBooks

A different approach to creating a dashboard in QuickBooks is available, as was mentioned in the section before this one. With a custom dashboard, you may expand QuickBooks' features and abilities to suit the particular requirements of your company. We illustrate a sample dashboard made outside of QuickBooks Online in the example below. The above custom dashboard was made using Coupler.io's automated data export functionality, which was then used to make graphs in a spreadsheet app or data visualization tool.

A third-party solution called Coupler.io enables you to automatically supply a wide range of data elements related to your QuickBooks analytics bars and graphs. You can extract a lot of information from receipts for sales, payments, bills, refunds, and other transactions.

To export your QuickBooks data, you must follow these steps after signing up for Coupler.io:

- Select the applications for source and destination when exporting QuickBooks data.

You must select QuickBooks as your source application. QuickBooks Reports are also included in the list. These reports are also a source of information for QuickBooks graphs. The list of available destination apps includes BigQuery, Microsoft Excel, and Google Sheets. We'll decide to use Microsoft Excel moving forwards. Access your QuickBooks account. Click Connect after signing into your QuickBooks Online account. Choosing a data category for exporting eight invoices. We chose to export the invoice data from the list of data entities. Your destination account to the network

Make your destination account settings. Following that, you will be prompted to choose an existing workbook and a current sheet. You can make a new sheet by entering a new name if you don't already have one. Additionally, the importer requests that you either place your newly imported data under previously imported entries or completely replace all previously imported data with the most recent import. The latter is appropriate for monitoring changes to historical data.

Create a unique schedule

The main function of Coupler.io is an automatic data refresh. The scheduling options are as follows:

- Time Period (Every Hour, Day, and Week)
- Weekday
- Time
- Time Zone

After completing this process, click *Save and Run*. The importer will next add data linked to invoices to the Excel sheet you designated as your Destination account. The outcome will resemble this:

It is possible to use these invoice-related details further. Coupler.io allows you to seamlessly combine past QuickBooks imports with data that is automatically exported from other QuickBooks entities. For instance, you currently have an Excel page with information on invoices. Information about customers is already available in different tabs, including balance and profit reports that have been imported into QuickBooks. A generic dashboard can incorporate all of this data. Additionally, each data collection will be refreshed with new data as soon as each importer runs again, keeping your dashboard current.

Use a no-code data integration to automate dataflows or hire our specialists to implement it for you. The QuickBooks data may be quickly fed into BI tools if you require more sophisticated visualization approaches. For instance, Google Sheets or BigQuery can be used as data sources for Google Data Studio, while Excel works seamlessly with Power BI.

Summary of the QuickBooks Online dashboard

To help you get the most out of QuickBooks Online, this section examines the dashboard in depth. The platform's aesthetically pleasing, and technically advanced dashboard significantly reduces the hassle of business bookkeeping. But as everyone who works in the finance industry is aware, it takes a lot of work to gather and organize data in order to create dashboards and generate insightful information. Despite the fact that QuickBooks offers a multitude of features and functionalities, using third-party solutions to create dashboards outside of QuickBooks could be a big-time saver and enable you to do more with your data.

Exploring the Menu Options

Main Navigation Menu

The main navigation menu in QuickBooks Online is the central hub that allows users to access various modules, features, and settings. It is the starting point for performing accounting tasks and managing financial data. Understanding the structure and options available in this menu is vital for efficient navigation through QuickBooks Online.

Upon logging into QBO, users will find the main navigation menu located on the left-hand side of the screen. The menu is organized in a hierarchical manner, with primary categories at the top level and subcategories and features nested under them. Let's explore the main components of the main navigation menu:

Dashboard

The Dashboard is the first option on the main navigation menu. It takes users back to the main dashboard, which provides an overview of the business's financial health. Users can see charts, graphs, and key financial data, such as income and expenses summaries, bank account balances, and accounts receivable and payable. The Dashboard is a useful starting point for assessing the company's current financial status and performance.

Transactions

Under the Transactions section, users will find essential features related to financial transactions:

- **Banking:** This option allows users to connect their bank and credit card accounts to QBO using bank feeds. Bank feeds automatically import and categorize transactions, making it easier to reconcile accounts and keep financial records up to date. Users can also manually upload bank statements for reconciliation.

- **Sales:** The Sales tab provides access to all sales-related activities, including creating and sending invoices to customers, recording sales receipts, and managing customer information. This section is crucial for tracking income and ensuring timely payments.
- **Expenses:** In the Expenses tab, users can record and categorize business expenses, manage vendor bills, and track other costs related to the business. Adequate expense tracking helps to manage expenditures and maintain accurate financial records.
- **Payroll:** For businesses with employees, the Payroll section is essential. It allows users to set up and manage payroll, process paychecks, and handle payroll taxes and forms. Proper payroll management ensures employees are paid both promptly and accurately.

Sales Tax

The Sales Tax section is where users can set up and manage sales tax rates and rules. QuickBooks Online automatically calculates sales tax on sales transactions based on the configured rates and rules. This feature is especially crucial for businesses that need to charge and remit sales tax.

Reports

The Reports section provides a wealth of financial and accounting reports that offer insights into the company's performance. Users can generate reports such as Profit and Loss (P&L) statements, Balance Sheets, Cash Flow reports, and various other financial analyses. Reports help users make informed business decisions, identify areas for improvement, and prepare for tax reporting.

Workers

The Workers section is where users can manage their employees and contractors. It allows for employee record management, contractor payments, and the generation of related reports. Properly maintaining worker records ensures compliance with labor laws and simplifies tax reporting.

Taxes

The Taxes section provides access to various tax-related features. Users can set up and manage tax rates, view tax liabilities, and prepare and file tax forms directly from QuickBooks Online. This section streamlines the tax preparation and filing process, saving time and reducing the risk of errors.

Accounting

The Accounting section contains essential accounting features and tools:

- **Chart of Accounts:** The Chart of Accounts is a comprehensive list of all the accounts used to record financial transactions in QBO. Users can add, edit, or delete accounts to customize their financial reporting.
- **Reconcile:** The Reconcile feature helps users match their bank and credit card transactions with entries in QuickBooks Online. This process ensures that all transactions are accurately recorded and accounted for.
- **Registers:** Registers display individual transactions for each account in a ledger-like format. Users can review and edit transaction details directly from the registers.
- **Currencies:** For businesses dealing with multiple currencies, this feature allows the setting up and management of foreign currencies, enabling accurate financial reporting in different currencies.

Sales Center

The Sales Center section provides a consolidated view of sales-related activities and transactions. Users can see open and overdue invoices, unpaid bills, and recent sales receipts. This section helps users stay on top of their sales and revenue collections.

Expenses Center

The Expenses Center section provides an overview of outstanding bills and expenses. Users can see which bills are due and manage payment schedules. This feature is useful for maintaining healthy vendor relationships and managing cash flow.

Projects

The Projects section is where users can track and manage income, expenses, and profitability for specific projects or jobs. This feature is especially beneficial for businesses that deal with multiple projects simultaneously.

Apps

The Apps section allows users to explore and add third-party apps and integrations that extend QuickBooks Online functionalities. Users can find specialized apps for various industries, further customizing their QBO experience to suit specific business needs.

Other

Under the *Other* category, users can access additional features and settings:

- **Recurring Transactions:** This feature allows users to set up and automate recurring transactions, such as invoices and bills, saving time and effort on repetitive tasks.
- **Attachments:** Users can attach and store relevant documents and files to transactions, invoices, and other records within QuickBooks Online.
- **Audit Log:** The Audit Log tracks all the changes made to transactions and records, providing a detailed history of user activities within the software.
- **Import Data:** QuickBooks Online allows users to import data from other accounting software or spreadsheets, making the transition to QBO smoother.

Chapter 3

Setting Up Your QuickBooks Online Account

In today's fast-paced business environment, managing finances and bookkeeping is crucial for the success of any company. QuickBooks Online (QBO) is a powerful cloud-based accounting software that has become immensely popular among businesses of all sizes. In this chapter, we will delve into the essential steps of setting up your QuickBooks Online account, ensuring you have a solid foundation to manage your financial records efficiently and effectively.

Creating Your Company Profile

You may set up or modify your company information in QuickBooks Online by following our instructions. You'll discover how to choose the correct company type, update a number of physical and email addresses, and input your data for printing on tax documents, including Form 1099 and payroll tax returns.

We recommend you use your own copy of QuickBooks Online to follow along with this tutorial, which is the first in our free QuickBooks tutorial series. If you don't already have a subscription, you can pick between a three-month 50% discount offer or a 30-day free trial.

Step 1: Gather Company Information and Sign in to QuickBooks

Gather the fundamental company information before we start setting up your firm in QuickBooks Online. Although it's ideal to include as many items from this list as you can, adjustments can always be made later.

- Name of the company
- Address
- Email
- Website
- A digital version of the corporate logo
- EIN, the federal employer identification number
- A partnership or a sole proprietorship as a business form
- Cash-basis versus accrual-basis accounting

Log into your QuickBooks account now that you have your data. Choose Account and Settings from your dashboard by clicking the cogwheel in the top-right corner of the screen. To access the Company tab, go to Account and Settings. Next, choose the Company tab from the Account and Settings section. There are five fields you must fill out on the Company tab: Company name, Company type, Contact information, Address, and Marketing Preferences. The company tab displays the areas you need to configure, such as the name, category, and contact information.

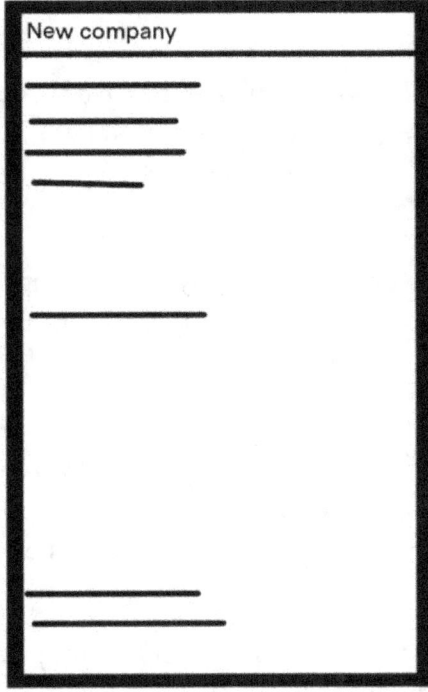
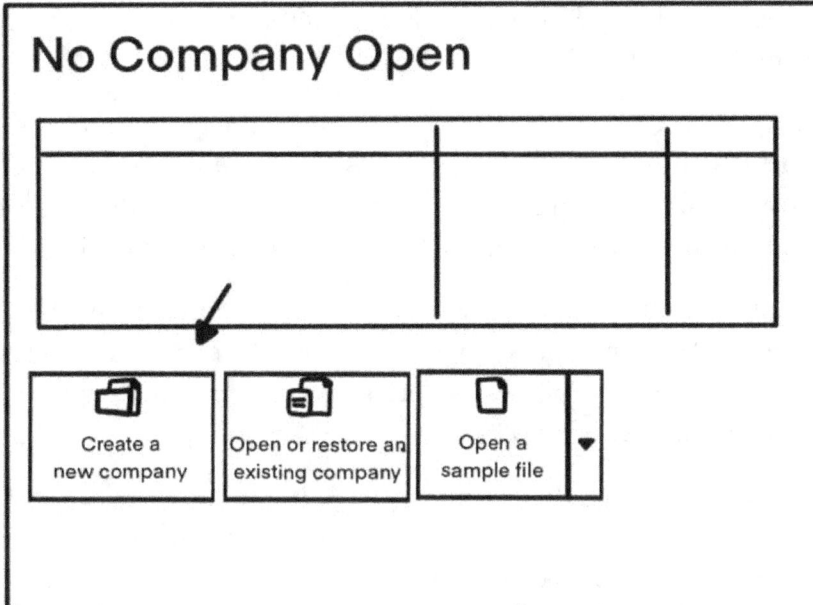

Step 2: Edit the Company Name

To modify the information, click anywhere in the firm name section, including on the pencil symbol. Click *Save* after making the necessary adjustments. The area where you can upload your logo, update the firm name, and enter your employer ID number is in the company name area.

In QuickBooks Online, change the company name, company logo, and EIN. As seen in the illustration above, there are three components in the firm name section:

A. **Company logo:** To add your company's logo to forms that are unique to you, import it. You must store your logo on your computer as an image file. To upload your logo, click on the grey square. We have already supplied a company logo in the screenshot up top. Click the blue plus sign, choose the file, and then click *Save* to add another logo.

B. **Company and legal name:** Type your company's name exactly as you want it to appear on paperwork and invoices. Your official business name should match the name that the IRS lists for your company. On tax documents such as Form 1099 and payroll tax returns, the legal name will be used. Uncheck the box and enter your legal name if it differs from the firm name you wish to appear on your invoices.

C. **EIN:** This should coincide with the number the IRS has given you. Use your Social Security number if you're self-employed. Because EINs are private information, QuickBooks may ask you to verify your login before accessing or editing the EIN. Take care not to use your Social Security number. Self-employed taxpayers are permitted to use their Social Security number rather than an EIN, but we strongly advise against doing so. Once you have finished inputting your company name, logo, and EIN, click the green Save button.

Step 3: Select the Company Type

To input or modify your company-type information, click the pencil icon or anywhere in the Company Type section. If you're unsure, you can leave the box blank. Choose your taxable entity type from the drop-down menu next to the Tax Form field: If you are the only person in charge of your company, you are a sole proprietor. Using Schedule C (Form 1040), you should disclose any income or losses. If you need help completing Schedule C, we have a tutorial for you.

If you're operating your firm with two or more partners, choose this business category. Partnerships use Form 1065 to report their business profits and losses. Read our detailed directions on how to complete Form 1065.The S corporation (S-corp) A corporation that chooses to be an S-corp report on Form 1120S and transfers corporate income, loss, and taxes to its shareholders.

C corporation: A corporation that meets the requirements to be a C corporation is taxed separately from its owners rather than via the owners. C-corps file reports using Form 1120.Nonprofit organization: Nonprofits are tax-exempt businesses that prioritize advancing social goals over making a profit. To report their annual activity, they use Form 990.

Company with limited liability (LLC): If you're not sure whether to file taxes as a single proprietor, partnership, or S-corp, choose this company structure. In the Industry section, begin typing your industry's name, and QuickBooks will offer choices. Unless you choose to leave it blank, you must select an industry from the QuickBooks list. When you're done, press the green Save button.

Step 4: Update your Contact Information

To enter contact details for QuickBooks and your clients, click anywhere in the Contact Info section, including the pencil symbol. This screen in QuickBooks Online allows you to edit your contact information. Your contact information can be added or modified in QuickBooks Online.

Email: QuickBooks will contact the QuickBooks administrator using the company email on file. Your clients' sales forms, like invoices, will include the customer-facing email address. Uncheck the option and enter the proper address if this is different from the QuickBooks administrator's email address.

Business phone: Type the phone number that will be on the sales forms delivered to consumers.

Website: Provide a URL that will be shown on all of your sales forms. When you're finished and prepared to begin inputting your company's address information, click the green Save button.

Step 5: Edit Your Company Address

To input or modify your company's address information, click the pencil icon or any other location in the address area. The corporate address, customer-facing address, and legal address all show in different areas in the most recent edition of QuickBooks Online. Fill out or modify your addresses in QuickBooks Online.

Company address: The company address, which serves as the business's physical address, is what you use to send payments to QuickBooks. Click *Save* after making the necessary adjustments.

Contact information for clients: This address, which can be seen on your invoices and other sales documents, should be where clients should send their payments. Uncheck the box and input the right customer-facing address if it differs from your corporate address. For modifications to be saved, click *Save*.

Official address: Your tax filings must be sent to the legal address, which must coincide with the address you have on record with the IRS. Again, you must uncheck the option and provide the legal address if this is different from the company address. Click the green Save button once you are pleased with the address you have provided.

Step 6 (Optional)

The last component lets you customize your marketing settings using QuickBooks, our top choice for the finest small business accounting software, which is owned by Intuit. You will be directed to Intuit's website if you click Marketing Preferences, where you will be prompted with a series of questions about how you would like to be contacted by Intuit. You can choose not to receive any mail, calls, or emails from Intuit by completing the survey.

How Do I Back Up My QuickBooks Data?

Backing up your data is crucial for any software, especially for accounting software like QuickBooks Online (QBO). Regular backups ensure that your financial data is safe and can be restored in case of any unforeseen issues, such as data corruption, accidental deletions, or other technical problems.

QuickBooks Online operates in the cloud, which means that all your data is stored online on Intuit's servers. This offers a level of security and backup that traditional desktop software might not provide. However, it's still a good practice to understand how backups work with QBO and how you can ensure your data's safety.

Backing Up Data in QuickBooks Online

Automatic Backups by Intuit

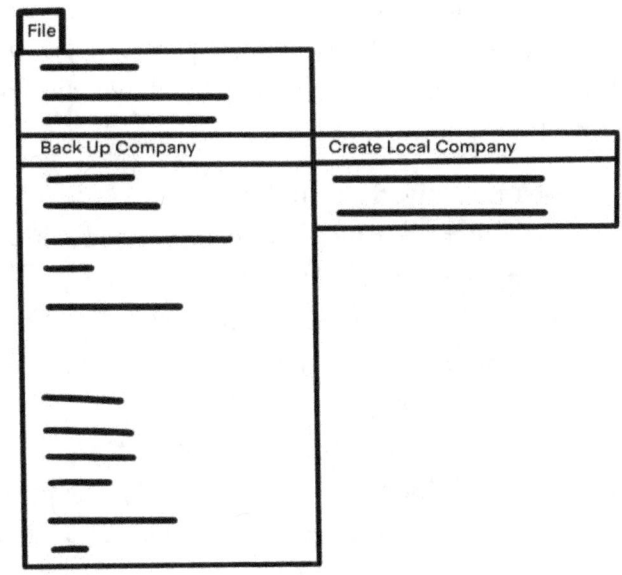

- QuickBooks Online automatically backs up your data every few minutes to ensure that even if you lose connection or face any other issues, your data remains safe.
- Intuit keeps your data backed up and protected with the same encryption technology used by the world's top banking institutions.
- Intuit retains your data backups for a period, allowing you to restore data from a particular point if needed.

Manual Backups

- While QBO doesn't offer traditional backup files like the desktop version, you can manually backup your data by exporting reports and lists.
- Go to the *Reports* section and export all necessary reports as PDFs.
- Export your lists (like Customers, Vendors, Products, and Services) to Excel.
- Regularly download and save your attachments, if any.

Third-Party Backup Solutions

- There are third-party applications available in the QuickBooks App Store that can help you backup your QBO data. These apps can automate the backup process and store data in a secondary location for added security.
- Before choosing a third-party solution, ensure it is reputable, read reviews, and understand its backup and restore processes.

Exporting Data to QuickBooks Desktop

- As an added measure, QBO allows you to export your company file to QuickBooks Desktop. This can serve as a backup but remember that there might be some data or feature discrepancies between the two versions.

Restoring Data

- If you ever need to restore your data, contact QuickBooks Online support. They can help you revert your data to a previous state, but this is typically limited to a specific timeframe.
- If you've used a third-party backup solution, follow their specific restoration process.

Integrating QBO with Other Software or Applications

In today's interconnected digital landscape, seamless integration between different software and applications is crucial for maximizing efficiency and productivity. QuickBooks Online provides integration with numerous third-party applications, which allows you to streamline your business operations and improve teamwork.

1. Go to the App Store in QBO:
   - Inside QBO, there's a section called Apps. Click on it.
2. Find the Program You Want:
   - Look for the software or app you want to connect with QBO.
   - You can use the search bar to type its name and find it faster.
3. Click on the App:
   - Once you find the app, click on it.
4. Follow the Steps:
   - The app will have instructions on how to connect it with QBO. Just follow those steps.
5. Done!
   - Once you've followed the steps, the app should now work with QBO.

Converting QuickBooks Desktop Data to QBO

Converting QuickBooks Desktop Data to QuickBooks Online (QBO) is a critical process for businesses seeking to transition from a locally installed accounting software to a cloud-based platform. It ensures that historical financial data, customer information, vendor records, and other essential details seamlessly transfer to the new system, allowing for continuity in financial management. While the conversion process is designed to be as comprehensive as possible, it is essential to be aware of what data will convert successfully and what data will not.

The Conversion Process

QuickBooks provides a built-in conversion tool that simplifies the process of moving data from QuickBooks Desktop to QuickBooks Online. The steps below outline the typical conversion process:

- **Preparation:** Before initiating the conversion, ensure that your QuickBooks Desktop data file is up-to-date and free from any errors. Run necessary reports to verify the accuracy of your financial records.
- **Sign in to QuickBooks Online:** Log in to your QuickBooks Online account and navigate to the Gear icon in the top right corner. From the drop-down menu, select *Import Data*.
- **Upload Data File:** Select the option to import data from QuickBooks Desktop. Follow the on-screen instructions to upload your QuickBooks Desktop data file (with the extension. QBW).
- **Mapping Data:** After the data file is uploaded, QuickBooks Online will guide you through a mapping process, where you match the accounts and items in your QuickBooks Desktop file to the corresponding ones in QuickBooks Online. This step ensures that the data is organized correctly in the new system.
- **Start the Conversion:** Once the mapping is complete, initiate the conversion process. QuickBooks Online will automatically migrate the convertible data from your QuickBooks Desktop file to your QBO account.

Convertible Data

The conversion process is generally successful in transferring a significant portion of your QuickBooks Desktop data to QuickBooks Online. The following data is considered convertible and will be moved to your QBO account:

- **Company Information:** Details such as your company name, address, contact information, and tax identification number will be carried over to QuickBooks Online.
- **Chart of Accounts:** Your existing chart of accounts in QuickBooks Desktop will be transferred to QuickBooks Online. This includes your income and expense accounts, assets, liabilities, and equity accounts.
- **Customer and Vendor Lists:** Customer and vendor records, including contact information, addresses, and payment terms, will convert to QuickBooks Online.
- **Open Transactions:** Open transactions, such as unpaid invoices, bills, and purchase orders, will be migrated to QuickBooks Online, ensuring you continue to have access to your outstanding financial commitments.

- **Products and Services:** Items and services you sell, along with their descriptions and prices, will be converted, allowing you to continue invoicing and tracking sales seamlessly.

Non-Convertible Data

While the conversion process is comprehensive, there are certain types of data that QuickBooks Online cannot transfer automatically. This means you will need to handle them manually in your QBO account. The non-convertible data includes:

- **Payroll Information:** Employee payroll data, wage rates, and payroll taxes are not transferred during the conversion process. If you are using payroll in QuickBooks Desktop, you will need to set up payroll in QuickBooks Online separately.
- **Payroll Forms:** Payroll forms, such as W-2s and 1099s, will not convert to QuickBooks Online. You will need to recreate and refile these forms in the new system as needed.
- **Customized Templates:** Custom invoice templates and other forms customized in QuickBooks Desktop will not automatically transfer to QuickBooks Online. You will need to recreate any customized templates in QBO to maintain consistent branding and layout.
- **Some Reports:** Certain specialized reports available in QuickBooks Desktop may not be available in the same format in QuickBooks Online. You may need to adjust and generate these reports using the available reporting options in QBO.

Data Verification and Cleanup

After the conversion process, it is essential to verify the accuracy of your data in QuickBooks Online. Perform a thorough review of your financial records to ensure that all information has been transferred correctly. Address any discrepancies or errors promptly to avoid future issues with your financial reporting.

Chapter 4
Managing Financial Accounts

In any business, managing financial accounts is crucial for ensuring its smooth operation and long-term success. This process entails accurately organizing and documenting financial transactions, in addition to assessing the company's financial well-being. This chapter delves into the essential aspects of financial account management, with a primary focus on the Chart of Accounts and Bank and Credit Card Reconciliation.

The Chart of Accounts and How to Customize It

What is the Chart of Accounts?

The Chart of Accounts is a core feature of QuickBooks Online (QBO) and, in fact, any accounting system. Imagine it as the backbone of your business's financial records. It's a structured list that categorizes and organizes all the financial transactions your business makes. This list includes everything from the money you earn (income) to the money you spend (expenses), the assets you own (like equipment or vehicles), and the money you owe (liabilities).

Why is the Chart of Accounts Important?

- **Financial Clarity:** The Chart of Accounts provides a clear and organized view of your business's financial activities. By looking at it, you can quickly understand where your money is coming from and where it's going.

- **Reporting:** When you want to generate financial reports, such as profit and loss statements or balance sheets, QBO pulls data from your Chart of Accounts. The clearer and more organized your Chart of Accounts is, the more accurate and insightful your reports will be.
- **Tax Preparation:** When tax season arrives, a well-maintained Chart of Accounts makes it easier to identify deductible expenses and report accurate income, ensuring you pay the right amount of tax.
- **Decision Making:** With a clear picture of your financial health, you can make informed decisions about investing in new equipment, hiring staff, or expanding your business.

Customizing the Chart of Accounts for Your Industry

Every industry has its unique financial nuances. A retail store's financial activities differ from those of a consulting firm or a restaurant. That's why customizing the Chart of Accounts to fit your specific industry is crucial.

- **Starting Point:** When you first set up QBO, it offers a default Chart of Accounts based on the industry you select. This is a great starting point, but it's often necessary to tweak it to fit your business perfectly.
- **Adding Accounts:** As your business evolves, you might venture into new areas. For instance, if you run a cafe and decide to start selling branded merchandise, you'd add a new income account for *Merchandise Sales*.
- **Removing or Hiding Unused Accounts:** Not every default account will be relevant to your business. If there's an account you never use, you can either delete it or make it inactive to declutter your Chart of Accounts.
- **Renaming Accounts:** The default names might not always resonate with your business's terminology. Feel free to rename them. For example, if you're in the tech industry, instead of *Product Sales*, you might prefer *Software Sales*.
- **Organizing Hierarchically:** QBO allows you to create parent accounts and sub-accounts. This is especially useful for businesses with diverse income streams or expenses. For instance, under a parent account named *Marketing Expenses*, you could have sub-accounts like *Digital Advertising*, *Print Advertising*, and *Event Sponsorships*.

Difference Between Accountant View and Business View

You have a choice between the Accountant View and the Business View in QuickBooks Online. The view you pick may affect how you access the task's command, even though you can largely do the same actions in both ways. The names of the links for the Navigation Bar commands are just one example of the interface changes that take place while switching between views.

In QuickBooks Online, the Accountant View offers a comprehensive list of business and accounting duties. As an alternative, QuickBooks Online Business View streamlines the view to concentrate on routine business operations. Unless otherwise specified by the lesson, we use the Accountant View for the purposes of our QuickBooks Online course. Click the *Settings* button in the QuickBooks Online toolbar in the top-right corner of the screen to switch between Accountant View and Business View. Then, to go to the opposite view from the current view, click the toggle option labeled *Switch to Business View/Switch to Accountant View* in the menu's lower-right corner. When you click on this link, the name of the view opposite the one you're presently working in will always change. As a result, when working actively in Accountant View, the link reads Switch to Business View. The title of the interface you're working in is displayed in the text to the left of this link.

How to Switch Between Accountant View and Business View

- Click the *Settings* button in the QuickBooks Online toolbar in the top-right corner of the screen to switch between Accountant View and Business View.
- Then, to go to the opposite view from the current view, click the toggle option labeled *Switch to Business View/Switch to Accountant View* in the menu's lower-right corner.
- When you click on this link, the name of the view opposite the one you're presently working in will always change.
- The name of the view you are currently using is also shown in the text that appears to the left of this link.

Adding, Editing, and Deleting Accounts

In QuickBooks Desktop for Windows and Mac, find out how to add, amend, or remove accounts from your chart of accounts. Upon creating a company file, QuickBooks automatically inserts relevant accounts into your chart of accounts tailored to your business needs to more effectively monitor your business's financial status, including assets, liabilities, and income, you can modify existing accounts or create new ones.

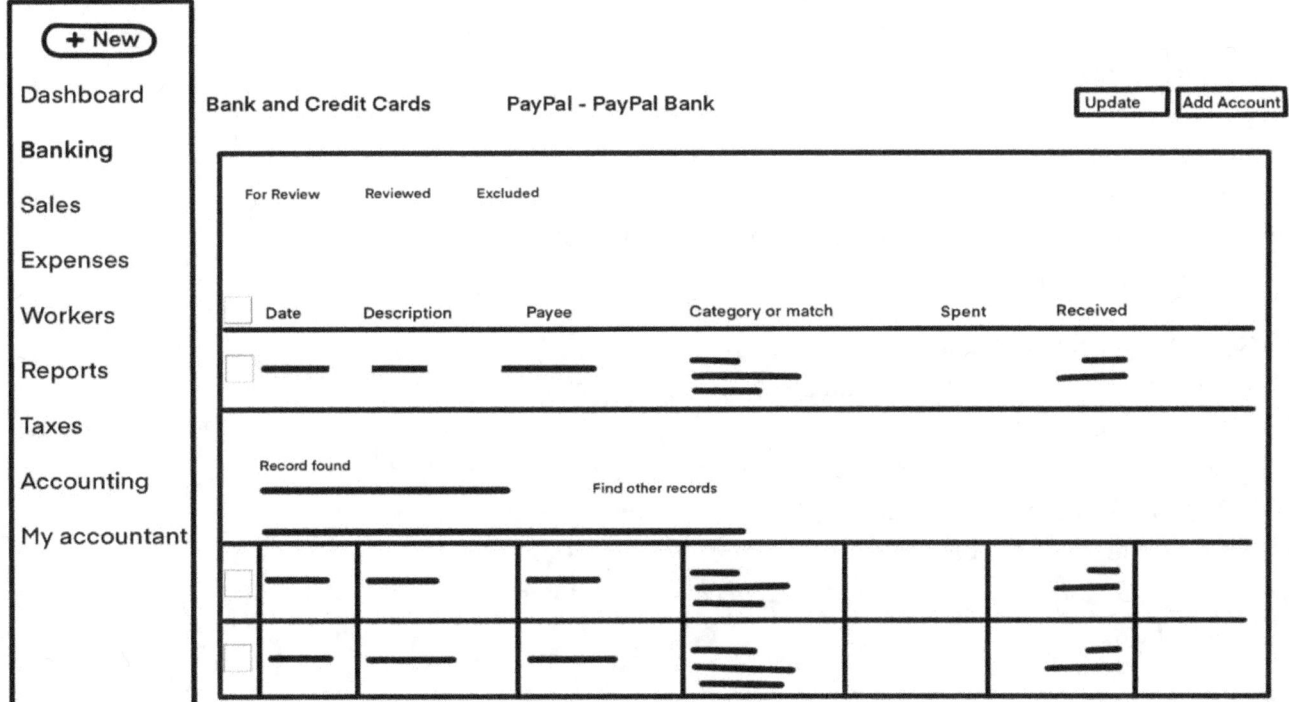

Add An Account

Should you need to monitor various transaction types, it's possible to incorporate additional accounts. You can add the following account types to your QuickBooks chart of accounts:

Desktop QuickBooks for Windows
1. A chart of accounts can be found by selecting *Lists* from the menu.
2. Select *New* from the Account dropdown menu.
3. Then click *Continue* after choosing an account type.
4. Fill out the account information.
5. Then *Save & Close* option.

Desktop QuickBooks for Mac
1. A chart of accounts can be found by selecting *Lists* from the menu.
2. Select *Create +*.
3. Select the account type from the *Type* drop-down menu.
4. Fill out the account information. Select *OK*.

Add a Subaccount

In order to keep track of particular accounts under a parent or main account, you may also add subaccounts. Your utility account (parent), for instance, has subaccounts for various utility costs like gas, phone, and water. Note: The account types of the parent and subaccount must match.

Desktop QuickBooks for Windows
1. A chart of Accounts can be found by selecting *Lists* from the menu.
2. Select *New* from the *Account* dropdown menu.
3. Then click *Continue* after choosing an account type.
4. Type in the account information.
5. Select the checkbox next to *Subaccount*.
6. Select the parent account from the *Subaccount* dropdown.
7. Then *Save & Close* option.

Desktop QuickBooks for Mac
1. A chart of Accounts can be found by selecting *Lists* from the menu.
2. Select *Create +*.
3. Select the account type from the *Type* drop-down menu.
4. Type in the account information.
5. Select the checkbox next to *Subaccount*.
6. Select the parent account from the *Subaccount* dropdown.
7. Select *OK*.

Edit an Account

You can alter an account's type, account number, description, and tax-line mapping if necessary.

Desktop QuickBooks for Windows

1. A chart of Accounts can be found by selecting *Lists* from the menu.
2. Select the account you want to update with the right click.
3. Decide on *Edit Account*.
4. Change the account information.
5. Then *Save & Close* option.

Desktop QuickBooks for Mac

1. A chart of Accounts can be found by selecting *Lists* from the menu.
2. Choose the account that needs editing.
3. Decide on *Editing*.
4. Change the account information.
5. Select *OK*.

Delete an Account

Should an account become unnecessary, you can remove it to maintain an orderly chart of accounts. Bear in mind, an account can only be deleted if there are no subaccounts linked to it. You must first remove any subaccounts, if present, or reassign them to a different primary account before deletion is possible. You haven't connected it to any items or used it in any transactions. If you're unable to delete the account, set it as inactive in your chart of accounts.

Desktop QuickBooks for Windows

1. A chart of Accounts can be found by selecting *Lists* from the menu.
2. Select the account you want to update with the right click.
3. Then click *Delete Account* and *OK*.

Desktop QuickBooks for Mac

1. A chart of Accounts can be found by selecting *Lists* from the menu.
2. To delete an account, select it.
3. Select *Delete Account* from the Edit menu.
4. Select OK.

Make an Account Inactive

If you are unable to delete an account, you can render it inactive. Your chart of accounts and transaction forms will no longer show the account as it is hidden. To ensure their accuracy, inactive accounts nonetheless show up in your reports.

Desktop QuickBooks for Windows

1. A chart of Accounts can be found by selecting *Lists* from the menu.
2. Right – click on the account you wish to deactivate and select *Edit Account* from the drop-down menu.
3. Check the box next to *Account* is inactive.
4. Then *Save & Close* option.

You can make the account active whenever you're ready to use it once more.

1. A chart of Accounts can be found by selecting *Lists* from the menu.
2. Include the inactive checkbox selected.
3. Right-click on the account you wish to reactivate and select *Edit Account* from the drop-down menu.
4. Uncheck the box that says Account is inactive.
5. Then *Save & Close* option.

Desktop QuickBooks for Mac
1. A chart of Accounts can be found by selecting *Lists* from the menu.
2. Select the account you wish to deactivate.
3. *Make Account Inactive* is the second option after selecting *Settings*.

You can reactivate the account whenever you decide to use it again:

1. A chart of Accounts can be found by selecting *Lists* from the menu.
2. Choose *All Accounts* from the *View* dropdown menu.
3. Select the account you wish to reactivate.
4. *Make Accounts Active* is the second option after choosing *Settings*.

Organizing Accounts

Organizing your accounts in QBO is essential for maintaining a clear and accurate view of your business's financial health. Properly structured accounts make it easier to record transactions, generate meaningful reports, and understand your financial position at a glance. Here's a guide to help you effectively organize your accounts:

Understand Account Types

Before organizing, it's crucial to understand the different types of accounts:

- **Income Accounts:** Track money coming into your business (e.g., sales, service fees).
- **Expense Accounts:** Track money going out of your business (e.g., rent, utilities, salaries).
- **Asset Accounts:** Represent what your business owns (e.g., cash, equipment, inventory).
- **Liability Accounts:** Represent what your business owes (e.g., loans, credit card balances).
- **Equity Accounts:** Show the owner's stake in the business.

Use Hierarchical Structure

QBO allows you to create parent accounts and sub-accounts. This is useful for categorizing related financial activities under one umbrella. For instance:

- **Parent Account:** Marketing Expenses
- **Sub-Account:** Digital Advertising
- **Sub-Account:** Print Advertising
- **Sub-Account:** Event Sponsorships

Rename Accounts for Clarity

The default names in QBO might not always fit your business's terminology. Rename accounts to terms that resonate with your operations. For example, instead of *Miscellaneous Income*, you might prefer *Consultation Fees*.

Remove or Hide Unused Accounts

To declutter your Chart of Accounts, make any irrelevant accounts inactive. This way, they won't appear in your regular view but will remain in the system for historical data.

Regularly Review and Update

As your business evolves, your financial activities might change. Regularly review your Chart of Accounts to add new relevant accounts or modify existing ones.

Use Account Numbers

Some businesses find it helpful to use account numbers for a more structured view. This can be especially useful for larger businesses with many accounts. If you decide to use account numbers, maintain a consistent numbering system.

Maintain Consistency

Whichever way you choose to organize, maintain consistency. This means using the same naming conventions, structures, and categorizations across all accounts. Consistency makes it easier for anyone reviewing the accounts to understand them.

Classifying Transactions

Learn how to classify the transactions you import into QuickBooks or download from your bank.

You must categorize each transaction that you enter into QuickBooks. This encompasses both transactions you input manually and those downloaded from an online banking account. QuickBooks places your transactions on the appropriate line of your Schedule C when you categorize. Additionally, it organizes your earnings and outgoings so you can see which components of your freelance business have the greatest influence.

Classify a Transaction

Through a web browser

1. Head over to the *Transactions* menu.
2. On the list, look for a transaction.
3. If the transaction was personal or business-related, choose *Business*.
4. Choose *Split* if both transactions were involved.
5. View the *Category* column to review the category.
6. QuickBooks makes an effort to classify your transactions.
7. Select the category link if you need to alter the category.

8. Choose a broad type, then a more specific category.
9. When finished, select *Save*.

On an iOS device (iPhone, iPad), an Android device (phone, tablet),
1. Go to the *Transactions* menu if you're using an iOS device.
2. Tap the *Menu* icon on your Android device, and then select *Transactions*.
3. On the list, look for a transaction.
4. Swipe left to categorize it as either business or personal. Select the transaction, then choose *Split* if the transaction combines both.
5. Review the category QuickBooks has chosen in the banner as you swipe.
6. Select the category link if you need to alter the category. Then select a different category.
7. You can easily categorize frequent spending and income by creating and managing category rules.

Change Or Reclassify a Transaction

Through a web browser
1. Head over to the *Transactions* menu.
2. Locate the transaction that needs editing.
3. To expand the transaction, select the icon.
4. Add remarks, change the transaction's name, or include a receipt.
5. Click on the link in the *Type* or *Category* column to change the category
6. Choose a new category next.
7. When finished, select *Save*.

On an iOS device (iPhone, iPad), an Android device (phone, tablet),
1. Go to the *Transactions* menu if you're using an iOS device.
2. Select the menu icon on your Android device, then choose *Transactions*.
3. Choosing the Reviewed tab.
4. Select the transaction that needs editing.
5. Select *Edit*.
6. Modify the category or the specifics.
7. When finished, select *Save*.

Bank and Credit Card Reconciliation

Bank and credit card reconciliation is a vital process that ensures the accuracy and reliability of a company's financial records. It involves comparing and matching the transactions recorded in the company's financial management software with the corresponding entries in the bank and credit card statements.

By performing regular reconciliations, businesses can identify and resolve discrepancies promptly, maintain data integrity, and gain a clear understanding of their true financial position. Here is a proper step-by-step procedure for conducting bank and credit card reconciliation:

Step 1: Gather the Necessary Information

Before starting the reconciliation process, gather all the essential information required for comparison. This includes the bank statements and credit card statements for the relevant period. Ensure that the statement periods match the accounting period being reconciled.

										Difference
$1,122.41				**$1,122.41**					✓	**$0.00**
$1,747.65			$2,645.24			$2,000.00				

Date	Cleared Date	Type	Red no.	Account	Payee	Memo	Payment	Deposit

Step 2: Access the Financial Management Software

Log in to the company's financial management software or accounting system with the appropriate credentials. Navigate to the section where bank and credit card transactions are recorded, typically under the *Banking* or *Transactions* tab.

Step 3: Connect Bank and Credit Card Accounts

Ensure that the bank and credit card accounts are connected to the financial management software. This connection allows for the automatic import of transactions, saving time and minimizing errors in data entry.

Step 4: Begin Reconciliation

Start the reconciliation process by selecting the bank account or credit card account you wish to reconcile. Choose the corresponding statement period, which should match the dates of the bank or credit card statement.

Step 5: Compare Transactions

Review each transaction recorded in the financial management software with the corresponding entry in the bank or credit card statement. Scrutinize transaction amounts, dates, and descriptions. Check for any discrepancies, such as missing or duplicate transactions.

Step 6: Mark Matched Transactions

As you compare each transaction, mark them as *matched* in the financial management software if they are accurately reflected in the bank or credit card statement. This indicates that the transactions are in agreement and have been properly recorded.

Step 7: Investigate and Resolve Discrepancies

If you encounter any discrepancies during the reconciliation process, investigate the reasons behind them. Common causes of discrepancies include timing differences (e.g., transactions that are pending or have not yet cleared), bank fees, errors in recording transactions, or fraudulent activities.

Step 8: Adjusting Entries

If discrepancies are identified, make the necessary adjusting entries in the financial management software. For example, if a transaction was recorded with the wrong amount or in the wrong account, correct it accordingly. Ensure that the changes are accurately reflected in both the software and the company's financial records.

Step 9: Reconcile to Zero

Continue marking transactions as *matched* and making adjustments until all discrepancies are resolved and the difference between the financial management software and the bank or credit card statement balances is zero. Reconciling to zero means that both sets of records agree and the accounts are balanced.

Step 10: Finalize the Reconciliation

Once the reconciliation is complete and the difference is zero, review the entire process to ensure accuracy. Save the reconciliation report and any supporting documents for future reference, especially during audits or financial reviews.

Step 11: Reconcile Regularly

For optimal financial management, it is essential to reconcile bank and credit card accounts regularly. Depending on the volume of transactions and the complexity of the business, reconciliations may be performed monthly, quarterly, or annually. Regular reconciliations help identify potential issues early, prevent errors from accumulating, and maintain the integrity of financial data.

Step 12: Continuous Monitoring and Improvement

After completing the reconciliation process, continuously monitor financial transactions and improve internal controls to minimize discrepancies and errors. Regularly assess the effectiveness of the reconciliation process and make necessary adjustments to enhance accuracy and efficiency.

By following this step-by-step procedure for bank and credit card reconciliation, businesses can maintain accurate financial records, ensure compliance with accounting standards, and make well-informed financial decisions. This process contributes to the overall financial stability and success of the company.

Chapter 5
Managing Customers and Sales

I n any business, managing customers and sales is of paramount importance. It involves not only maintaining accurate customer information but also streamlining the sales process for maximum efficiency. This chapter delves into various aspects of customer and sales management, providing comprehensive guidance on tasks such as adding and managing customer information, creating and sending invoices, tracking sales, recording payments, generating purchase orders, and creating estimates. By mastering these essential functions, businesses can enhance customer relationships, optimize sales processes, and ultimately drive overall growth and success.

Adding and Managing Customer Information

QuickBooks Online is a powerful cloud-based accounting software designed to streamline business finances and help manage customers and sales efficiently. In this procedure, we will explore step-by-step instructions on how to effectively manage customers and sales using QuickBooks Online.

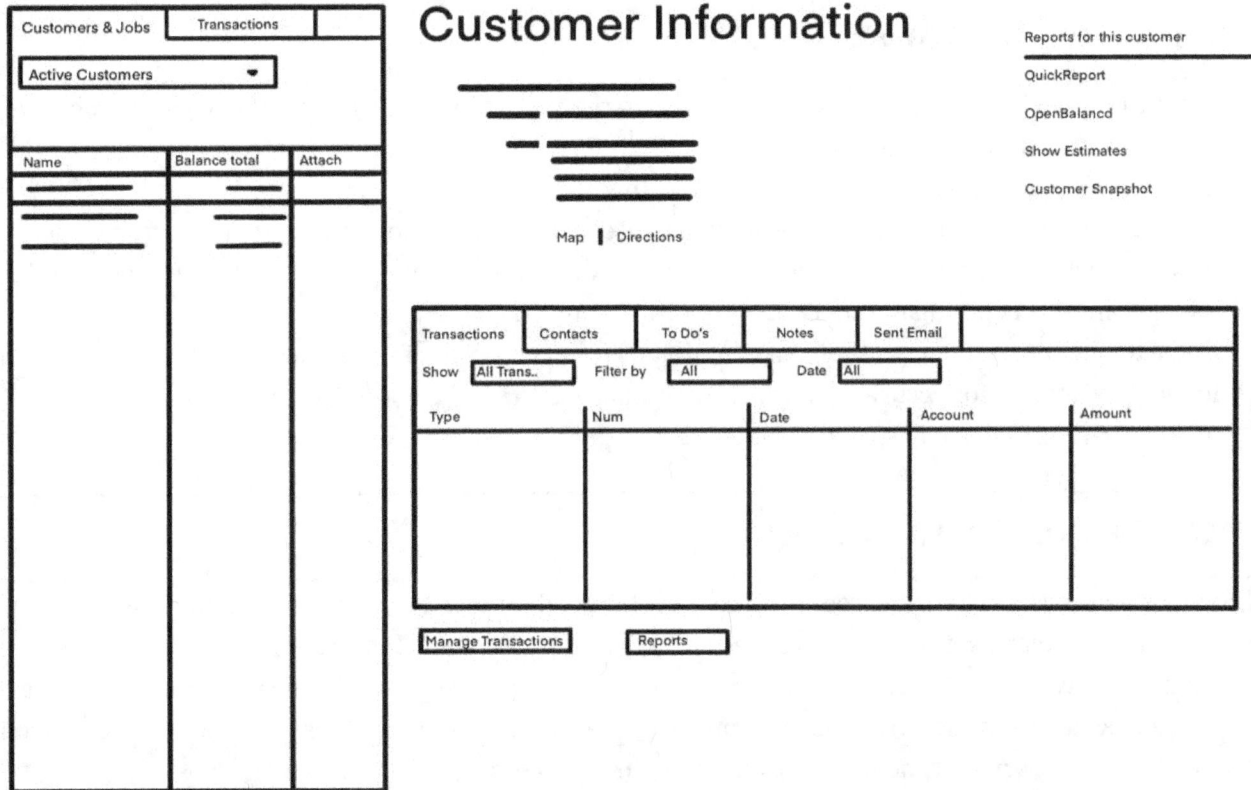

Step 1: Sign in to QuickBooks Online

1. Open your web browser and navigate to the QuickBooks Online login page.
2. Enter your username and password to log in to your QuickBooks Online account.

Step 2: Navigate to Customers

1. From the QuickBooks Online dashboard, click on the *Sales* tab located in the left-hand navigation menu.
2. Choose *Customers* from the menu options to navigate to the customer management area.

Step 3: Add a New Customer

1. Click on the *New Customer* button in the upper-right corner of the Customers page.
2. Fill in the required customer information, such as name, email, address, phone number, and any other relevant details.
3. Optionally, you can add additional information like payment terms, opening balance, and notes to provide more context about the customer.

Step 4: Edit Customer Information

1. To modify customer information, locate the customer from the list and click on their name to open the customer details page.
2. Press the *Edit* button located in the top-right corner to modify settings.
3. Update the necessary fields and click *Save* to save the changes.

Creating and Sending Invoices

1. From the QuickBooks Online dashboard, click on the Sales tab in the left-hand navigation menu.
2. Select *Invoices* from the drop-down menu.
3. Click on the *New Invoice* button to start a new invoice.
4. Choose the customer from the drop-down list or enter the customer's name in the *Customer* field.
5. Add products or services by typing their names in the *Product/Service* field, and QuickBooks Online will automatically populate the details if they exist in your inventory.
6. Enter the quantity and any other relevant details for each product or service.
7. Review the invoice for accuracy and click *Save and Send* to send the invoice directly to the customer's email or *Save and Close* to save it for later sending.

Creating Invoice Templates

By following this procedure, businesses can create customized invoice templates with labor and materials subtotals and an automatic service fee percentage in QuickBooks Online. This streamlined invoicing process eliminates manual work, improves efficiency, and ensures accurate and professional invoices are sent to customers. QuickBooks Online powerful customization features enable businesses to present clear and detailed invoices while saving time and effort in the billing process.

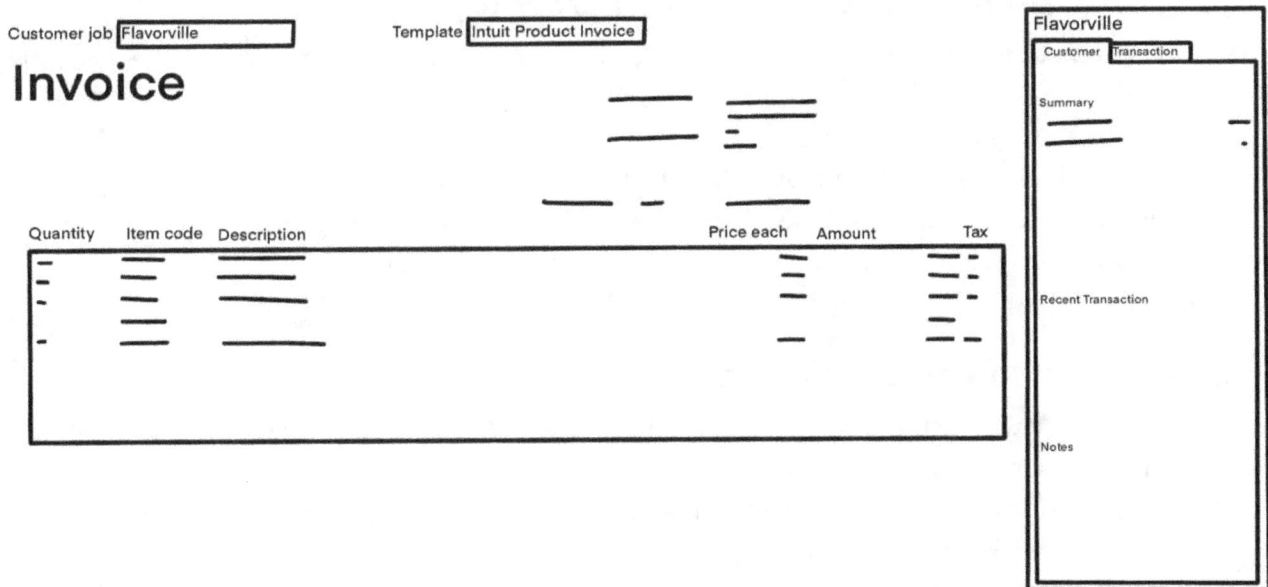

Step 1: Sign in to QuickBooks Online

1. Open your web browser and navigate to the QuickBooks Online login page.
2. Enter your username and password to log in to your QuickBooks Online account.

Step 2: Access Invoice Customization

1. From the QuickBooks Online dashboard, click on the *Sales* tab located in the left-hand navigation menu.
2. Select *Sales Forms* from the drop-down menu.
3. Click on the *Customize* button in the upper-right corner to access invoice customization options.

Step 3: Customize Invoice Template

In the customization interface, numerous settings are available to tailor your invoice template you will find various options to personalize your invoice template. These options include:

A. **Design:** Choose a color scheme and font style that aligns with your brand identity.
B. **Content:** Select the fields you want to include on the invoice, such as customer details, item details, labor, materials, and service fee.
C. **Layout:** Adjust the layout of the invoice to display information in a clear and organized manner.

Step 4: Add Labor and Materials Subtotals

1. To add labor and materials subtotals to the invoice template, go to the *Content* section in the customization window.
2. Click on the *Header* tab to add header information to the invoice template.
3. Click on the *Columns* tab and select *Subtotal* under the *Calculate* column for both labor and materials.
4. Click *Done* to save the changes.

Step 5: Set Up Automatic Service Fee Percentage

1. To automate the addition of a service fee percentage to each invoice, go back to the customization window.
2. Click on the *Content* section again.
3. Click on the *Footer* tab to add footer information to the invoice template.
4. Click on the *Calculations* tab and select *Percentage* under the *Calculate* column.
5. Enter the service fee percentage you want to apply to each invoice.
6. Click *Done* to save the changes.

Step 6: Save and Use the Customized Template

1. Once you have customized the invoice template with labor and materials subtotals and the automatic service fee, click *Done* to save the template.
2. To use the customized template when creating an invoice, click on the *+ New* button located at the top of the QuickBooks Online dashboard.
3. Select *Invoice* from the drop-down menu.
4. Choose the customer you are invoicing from the drop-down list or enter the customer's name in the Customer field.
5. Add products or services, and QuickBooks Online will automatically calculate the labor and materials subtotals based on the quantities and rates.
6. The service fee percentage you set up earlier will also be automatically applied to the total invoice amount.
7. Review the invoice for accuracy and click *Save and Send* to send the invoice directly to the customer's email or Save and Close to save it for later sending.

Tracking Sales and Managing Payments

QuickBooks Online provides robust tools for tracking sales and managing payments efficiently. This procedure outlines step-by-step instructions on how to effectively track sales, record income, and manage customer payments in QuickBooks Online.

Step 1: Sign in to QuickBooks Online

1. Open your web browser and navigate to the QuickBooks Online login page.
2. Input your login credentials, consisting of your username and password, to access your QuickBooks Online account.

Step 2: Access Sales Transactions

1. From the QuickBooks Online dashboard, click on the *Sales* tab located in the left-hand navigation menu.
2. Select *Sales* from the drop-down menu to access the sales transactions section.

Step 3: Create Sales Transactions

1. To record sales transactions such as invoices and sales receipts click on the *+ New* button in the upper-right corner of the Sales Transactions page.
2. Select *Invoice* or *Sales Receipt* from the drop-down menu, depending on the type of sales transaction you want to record.
3. Enter the customer's name or select an existing customer from the drop-down list.
4. Add products or services sold, along with quantities and rates, to calculate the total amount. Review the sales transaction for accuracy.
5. Click *Save and Send* to send the invoice directly to the customer's email or *Save and Close* to save it for later sending.

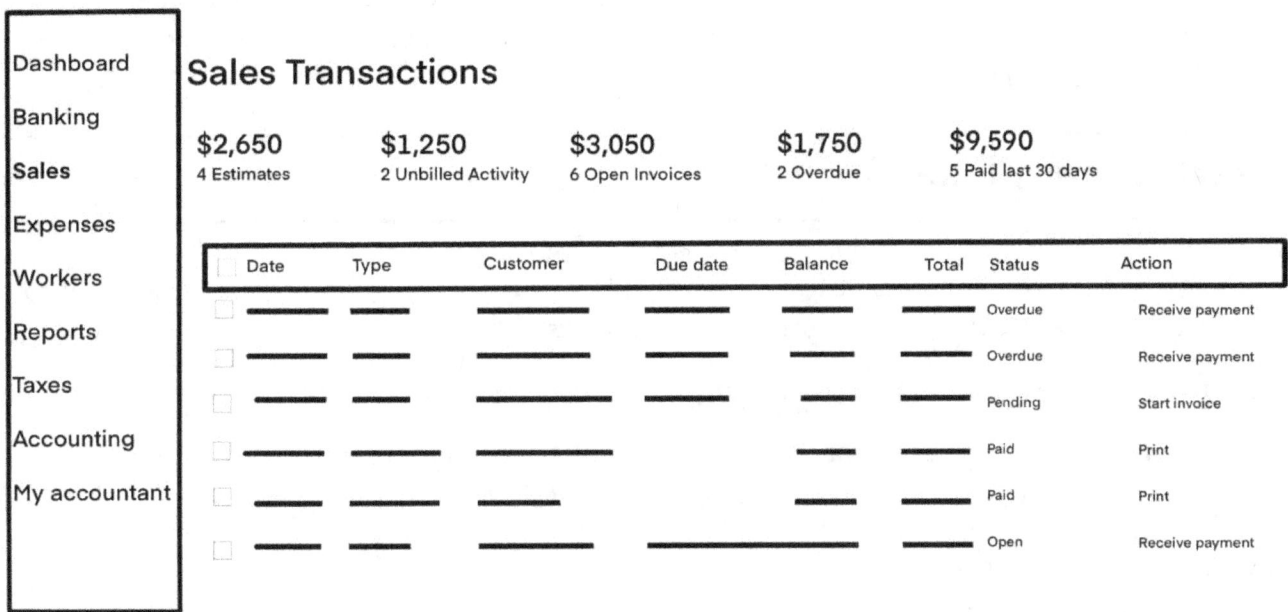

Step 4: Reconcile Bank Transactions

Regularly reconcile bank transactions with QuickBooks Online to ensure that all sales and payments are accurately reflected.

1. From the QuickBooks Online dashboard, click on the *Accounting* tab located in the left-hand navigation menu.
2. Select *Reconcile* from the drop-down menu.
3. Choose the bank account you wish to reconcile and enter the statement date and ending balance.
4. Follow the on-screen instructions to match and confirm transactions, ensuring that all sales and payments are accounted for.

Step 5: Run Sales Reports

1. Go to the *Reports* tab on the left-hand navigation menu.
2. Under the *Business Overview* section, select *Sales by Customer Summary* or *Sales by Product/Service Summary* to get an overview of sales performance.

3. Customize the report by selecting the desired date range, filters, and other parameters.
4. Click *Run Report* to generate the sales report.

Recording Payments

To record customer payments received:

1. Go to the *Sales* tab and select *Customers* from the drop-down menu.
2. Locate the customer for whom you want to record a payment and click on their name to open the customer details page.
3. Click the *Receive Payment* button in the upper-right corner.
4. Enter the payment details, including the payment date, payment method, and amount received. e. Optionally, apply the payment to specific invoices or leave it unapplied for later allocation.
5. Click *Save and Close* to record the payment.

Creating Purchase Orders

QuickBooks Online offers a straightforward process for creating purchase orders, enabling businesses to efficiently manage procurement and track orders with vendors. This procedure provides step-by-step instructions on how to create purchase orders in QuickBooks Online.

Step 1: Sign in to QuickBooks Online

1. Open your web browser and navigate to the QuickBooks Online login page.
2. Enter your username and password to log in to your QuickBooks Online account.

Step 2: Access Purchase Orders

1. From the QuickBooks Online dashboard, click on the *+ New* button located at the top of the page.
2. Select *Purchase Order* from the Suppliers section to access the purchase order creation screen.

Step 3: Choose Vendor and Order Details

1. In the purchase order creation screen, select the vendor from whom you want to place the order from the *Vendor* drop-down list. If the vendor does not appear in the list, select the *Add New* option to establish a new vendor profile.
2. Enter the purchase order date, expected delivery date, and purchase order number (optional but helpful for tracking).
3. Specify the shipping address and other relevant details in the appropriate fields.

Step 4: Add Items to the Purchase Order

1. In the *Item Details* section, enter the products or services you wish to order from the selected vendor.
2. Start typing the name of the product or service in the *Product/Service* field, and QuickBooks Online will suggest matching items from your inventory or products/services list.
3. Enter the quantity, rate, and any other necessary details for each item.
4. If you need to add more items to the purchase order, click the *+ Add lines* button.

Step 5: Review and Save the Purchase Order

1. After adding all the items to the purchase order, review the order details to ensure accuracy.
2. Double-check the vendor information, item quantities, and delivery dates.
3. If everything looks correct, click the *Save and send* button to save the purchase order and send it to the vendor directly from QuickBooks Online via email. Alternatively, click *Save and close* to save the purchase order without sending it immediately.

Step 6: Manage and Track Purchase Orders

1. To access the list of purchase orders, click on the *Expenses* tab located in the left-hand navigation menu.
2. Select *Purchase Orders* from the drop-down menu to view all created purchase orders.
3. From this list, you can easily filter, search, or edit any existing purchase orders as needed.

Step 7: Convert Purchase Orders to Bills or Vendor Invoices

1. Once the vendor delivers the products or services, you can convert the purchase order into a bill or vendor invoice for payment.
2. Go to the list of purchase orders and locate the relevant one.
3. Click the *Create bill* or *Create vendor invoice* button to generate the bill or vendor invoice using the information from the purchase order.

Creating Estimates

QuickBooks Online provides a simple and effective way to create estimates, also known as quotes or bids, for potential customers. Estimates allow businesses to provide detailed pricing information for products or services before finalizing a sale. This procedure outlines step-by-step instructions on how to create estimates in QuickBooks Online.

Step 1: Sign in to QuickBooks Online

1. Open your web browser and navigate to the QuickBooks Online login page.
2. Enter your username and password to log in to your QuickBooks Online account.

Step 2: Access Estimates

1. From the QuickBooks Online dashboard, click on the *+ New* button located at the top of the page.
2. Select *Estimate* from the Customers section to access the estimate creation screen.

Step 3: Choose Customer and Estimate Details

1. In the estimate creation screen, select the customer for whom you are creating the estimate from the *Customer* drop-down list. If the customer is not listed, click *Add New* to create a new customer profile.
2. Enter the estimate date, expiration date (optional but recommended), and estimate number (optional but helpful for tracking).
3. Optionally, you can add a custom message to the customer in the *Message on Estimate* field.

Step 4: Add Items to the Estimate

1. In the *Product/Service* column, start typing the name of the product or service you want to include in the estimate.
2. QuickBooks Online will suggest matching items from your inventory or products/services list.
3. Enter the quantity, rate, and any other necessary details for each item on the estimate.
4. If you need to add more items to the estimate, click the *+ Add lines* button.

Step 5: Customize Estimate Settings (Optional)

1. Click on the *Customize* button at the bottom of the estimate creation screen to access additional settings.
2. Here, you can customize the estimate form layout, design, and fields to match your business's branding and specific requirements.
3. Once you have made the desired customizations, click *Done* to save the changes.

Step 6: Review and Save the Estimate

1. After adding all the items to the estimate, review the estimate details to ensure accuracy.
2. Double-check the customer information, item quantities, and estimate expiration date.
3. If everything looks correct, click the *Save and send* button to save the estimate and send it directly to the customer via email. Alternatively, click *Save and new* to save the estimate without sending it immediately.

Step 7: Manage and Track Estimates

1. To access the list of estimates, click on the *Sales* tab located in the left-hand navigation menu.
2. Select *All Sales* from the drop-down menu and click on the *Estimates* tab to view all created estimates.
3. From this list, you can easily filter, search, or edit any existing estimates as needed.

Chapter 6
Inventory Management Basics

Effective inventory control is a fundamental component of running a successful business. It involves the process of efficiently handling and tracking the inventory or stock of products that a company buys, produces, or sells. Efficient inventory management ensures that a company can meet customer demand, avoid stockouts, minimize holding costs, and optimize cash flow. In the realm of modern businesses, where digital solutions have become the norm, QuickBooks Online stands out as one of the leading software platforms that streamline inventory management.

QuickBooks Online is an intuitive cloud-based accounting software developed by Intuit. It offers a range of tools and features to help businesses of all sizes manage their finances effectively. Within QuickBooks Online, inventory management plays a pivotal role in facilitating smooth operations for businesses dealing with physical products.

Dashboard	**Products and Services**									
Banking										
Sales										
Expenses		2 Low stock			4 Out of stock					
Workers										
Reports	Name	Sku	Type	Sales des	Sales price	Cost	Taxable	Qty on H	Reorder	Action
Taxes										
Accounting										
My accountant										

Setting Up Inventory Items and Tracking Quantities

Before delving into the intricacies of inventory management in QuickBooks Online, the first step is setting up inventory items and configuring the system to track quantities accurately. In the software, each product that a business sells or buys needs to be defined as an inventory item. To achieve this, users can access the inventory setup section and enter essential details for each item, such as the item name, description, SKU (Stock Keeping Unit), sales price, cost, and preferred vendor.

Tracking quantities is essential to understand the current stock levels of each item. QuickBooks Online offers a straightforward system where users can enter the quantity on hand for each inventory item, which gets updated automatically with every purchase or sale. This real-time tracking capability ensures that businesses always have an accurate idea of their inventory levels.

Recording Purchases and Tracking Inventory Costs

In any business that involves buying and selling products, keeping track of purchases and inventory costs is essential. QuickBooks Online allows users to record purchase transactions efficiently. When a purchase is made, users can enter the supplier's details, the inventory item purchased, the quantity bought, and the total cost.

The software then automatically updates the inventory quantity on hand and calculates the new average cost of each item. The average cost is a crucial metric used in inventory management, as it represents the cost at which items are both bought and sold.

Recording Purchases and Tracking Inventory Costs

Setting up Inventory Items

Before you can start recording purchases and tracking inventory costs in QuickBooks Online, you need to set up your inventory items. These items represent the products you buy and sell. To do this, follow these steps:

1. **Navigate to the Gear Icon:** Log in to your QuickBooks Online account and click on the Gear icon located in the upper-right corner of the dashboard.
2. **Choose Products and Services:** Under the *Lists* section, select *Products and Services*.
3. **Add New Item:** Click on the *New* button to add a new inventory item.
4. **Enter Item Details:** Fill in the necessary information for the item, including the name, SKU (Stock Keeping Unit), sales price, cost, and quantity on hand. You can also add a description and choose a category for better organization.
5. **Save the Item:** Once you have filled in the details, click *Save and Close* to save the inventory item.

Tracking Quantities

Now that you have set up your inventory items, it's essential to keep track of their quantities to avoid stockouts and overstocking. QuickBooks Online provides several methods to track inventory quantities, such as:

- **Automated Tracking:** If you enable the automatic tracking feature for inventory items, QuickBooks Online will adjust the quantities based on sales and purchase transactions.
- **Manual Tracking:** If you prefer manual control over your inventory, you can manually update the quantity on hand by editing the item details.

- **Barcode Scanning:** For businesses with a large inventory, QuickBooks Online supports barcode scanning, making it easier to track items and update quantities accurately.

Recording Purchases

Recording purchases of inventory items in QuickBooks Online helps maintain accurate records and provides valuable insights into your expenses. Here's how you can do it:

1. **Navigate to the Supplier Section:** From the dashboard, go to the *Supplier* section and click on *Expense* or *Supplier Credit* (whichever is applicable).
2. **Choose Supplier:** Select the supplier from whom you purchased the inventory items from the drop-down list.
3. **Select the Inventory Item:** Click on *Add a line* and choose the inventory item you purchased. Enter the quantity and cost per item.
4. **Review and Save:** Double-check the information for accuracy and then save the purchase transaction.

Managing Sales and Tracking Inventory Sales

Tracking Quantities

Once inventory items are set up, it is essential to keep track of the quantities on hand accurately. Tracking quantities helps in understanding stock levels, knowing when to reorder, and preventing stockouts or overstocking. QuickBooks Online provides tools to facilitate efficient quantity tracking:

Step 1: Viewing Inventory Status
1. From the Dashboard, click on *Sales* in the left-side menu and select *Products and Services*.
2. The Products and Services page displays a list of all inventory items, along with their respective quantities on hand.

Step 2: Updating Inventory Quantities
1. To add or deduct items from the inventory, click on an item from the list.
2. Click on the *Edit* button and update the *Quantity on hand* field.
3. Save the changes by clicking *Save and Close*.

Recording Purchases and Sales

Accurate recording of inventory purchases and sales is crucial for maintaining precise financial records and managing inventory efficiently. QuickBooks Online simplifies this process through the following steps:

Step 1: Recording Purchases
1. From the Dashboard, go to *Expenses* in the left-side menu and select *Supplier Expenses*.
2. Click on the *New transaction* button and choose *Bill* or *Expense* based on how the inventory was purchased.

For Bills:
1. Enter the supplier's details, bill date, and due date (if applicable).

2. Select the inventory item purchased, along with the quantity and cost.
3. Save the bill by clicking *Save and Close*.

For Expenses:
1. Choose the supplier and payment account.
2. Select the inventory item and enter the quantity and cost.
3. Save the expense transaction by clicking *Save and Close*.

Step 2: Recording Sales
1. From the Dashboard, go to *Sales* in the left-side menu and select *Invoices*.
2. Click on the *New transaction* button and choose *Invoice*.
3. Enter the customer's details and invoice date.
4. Select the inventory item sold, along with the quantity and sales price.
5. Save the invoice by clicking *Save and Close*.

Using Inventory Reports to Monitor Stock Levels

QuickBooks Online provides various inventory reports to help you analyze your inventory management and make informed business decisions. Some essential reports include:

- **Inventory Valuation Summary:** This report shows the total value of your inventory items, including the quantity on hand, cost, and total value.
- **Inventory Stock Status:** The stock status report displays the current quantity on hand for each inventory item, helping you identify items that may need reordering.
- **Sales by Product/Service Detail:** This report provides insights into the sales performance of each inventory item over a specific period.
- **Purchase by Product/Service Detail:** The purchase report helps you track the expenses related to acquiring inventory items.

Adjusting Inventory for Damaged or Lost Items

Inventory adjustments are necessary when goods become damaged, lost, or unsellable due to various reasons like theft or spoilage. QuickBooks Online simplifies this process, enabling businesses to adjust their inventory quantities accurately.

To adjust inventory for damaged or lost items:

1. On the QuickBooks Online dashboard, select *Sales* from the left-hand menu.
2. Choose *Products and Services* to view the list of your inventory items.
3. Find the item that requires an adjustment and click on the drop-down arrow next to it.
4. Select *Adjust Quantity*.
5. Enter the adjustment date and choose the appropriate reason for the adjustment (e.g., *Damaged* or *Lost*).

6. Enter the quantity you wish to adjust (subtract the damaged or lost items from the existing quantity).
7. Choose the appropriate account for the adjustment (e.g., *Loss on Inventory* or *Cost of Goods Sold*).
8. Save the inventory adjustment.

Understanding The Cost of Goods Sold (COGS) Calculation

Costs of producing Product X are as below:

Direct Raw Material:	$500,000
Direct Labour:	$100,000
Overhead Expenses:	$500,000
Opening Inventory:	$250,000
Closing Inventory:	$125,000
COGS	=C5+C2+C3-C6

COGS = Opening Inventory+ Purchases - Closing Inventory

Please Note: COGS does not include indirect expenses. Hence Overhead expenses have not been included in calculation of COGS above.

Cost of Goods Sold (COGS) is a vital financial metric that represents the direct costs of producing or purchasing the goods sold by a company during a specific period. Calculating COGS accurately is essential for determining the true profitability of a business. In QuickBooks Online, COGS calculation involves two methods: Average Cost and FIFO (First-In-First-Out). Let's explore each method in detail:

Average Cost Method

The Average Cost method calculates COGS by taking the average cost of all units of inventory available for sale during a given period. Here's how it works:

Assigning Average Cost

In this method, QuickBooks Online automatically assigns an average cost to each unit of inventory based on the total cost of available inventory and the number of units.

COGS Calculation

To calculate COGS using the Average Cost method, QuickBooks Online multiplies the number of units sold by the average cost per unit.

COGS = Number of Units Sold x Average Cost per Unit

Example

Suppose a company has 100 units of a product with a total cost of $1,000. The average cost per unit would be $1,000/100 = $10. If 20 units are sold during a specific period, the COGS would be 20 x $10 = $200.

FIFO (First-In-First-Out) Method

The FIFO method is based on the assumption that the first units of inventory, whether purchased or manufactured, are the first to be sold. This method aligns with the actual flow of inventory and is widely used in businesses with perishable or time-sensitive products. Here's how it works:

Tracking Inventory Acquisition

In the FIFO method, QuickBooks Online tracks each inventory acquisition, noting the date and cost of each purchase.

COGS Calculation

To calculate COGS using the FIFO method, QuickBooks Online takes the cost of the oldest (first) units available in inventory and multiplies that cost by the number of units sold.

COGS = Number of Units Sold x Cost of Oldest Units

Example

Suppose a company makes three inventory purchases of a product:

- Purchase 1: 50 units at $5 each
- Purchase 2: 30 units at $7 each
- Purchase 3: 20 units at $6 each

If 20 units are sold during the specific period, according to the FIFO method, the COGS would be calculated based on the cost of the oldest units, which are the 50 units purchased at $5 each.

COGS = 20 units x $5 per unit = $100

Performing Inventory Reconciliations

Reconciling your inventory records ensures that your physical stock matches the data in QuickBooks Online. Regular reconciliations help identify discrepancies, such as lost or damaged items and maintain the accuracy of your financial records. The reconciliation process involves physically counting your inventory and adjusting any discrepancies in the software.

To perform reconciliations:

1. Schedule regular inventory counts to compare physical stock with QuickBooks Online records.
2. Note any discrepancies between the actual count and the recorded quantity.
3. Create an inventory adjustment in QuickBooks Online for each discrepancy.
4. On the QuickBooks Online dashboard, select *Sales* from the left-hand menu.
5. Choose *Products and Services* to view the list of your inventory items.
6. Find the item with a quantity discrepancy and click on the drop-down arrow next to it.

7. Select *Adjust Quantity*.
8. Enter the adjustment date, quantity on hand, and the new quantity you counted.
9. Choose the appropriate account for the adjustment (e.g., *Loss on Inventory* or *Inventory Shrinkage*).
10. Save the inventory adjustment.

Chapter 7

Vendor and Expenses Management

In the ever-evolving world of business, effective vendor and expenses management stands as a pillar of success for any organization. In this chapter, we delve into the crucial aspects of handling vendor information, recording expenses, tracking bills, managing payments, and accessing payment history. Furthermore, we explore the significance of quotes, estimates, and job costing in streamlining business operations.

Adding and Managing Vendor Information

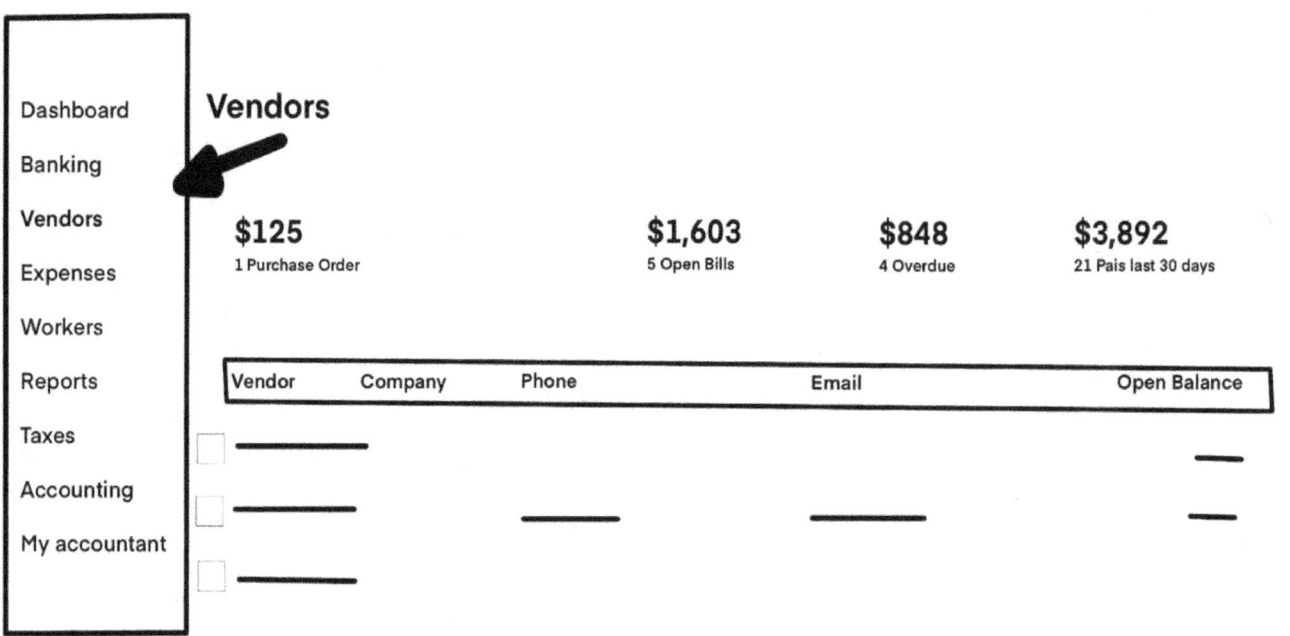

Before diving into the procedures, it is essential to grasp the concept of vendor management and its significance in the accounting process. Vendors, also commonly called suppliers, are companies or people who provide services or products to other companies. Managing vendors involves maintaining a centralized database of vendor information, keeping track of transactions with them, and ensuring timely payments. QuickBooks Online streamlines this process by providing a user-friendly platform for seamless vendor management.

Adding Vendor Information

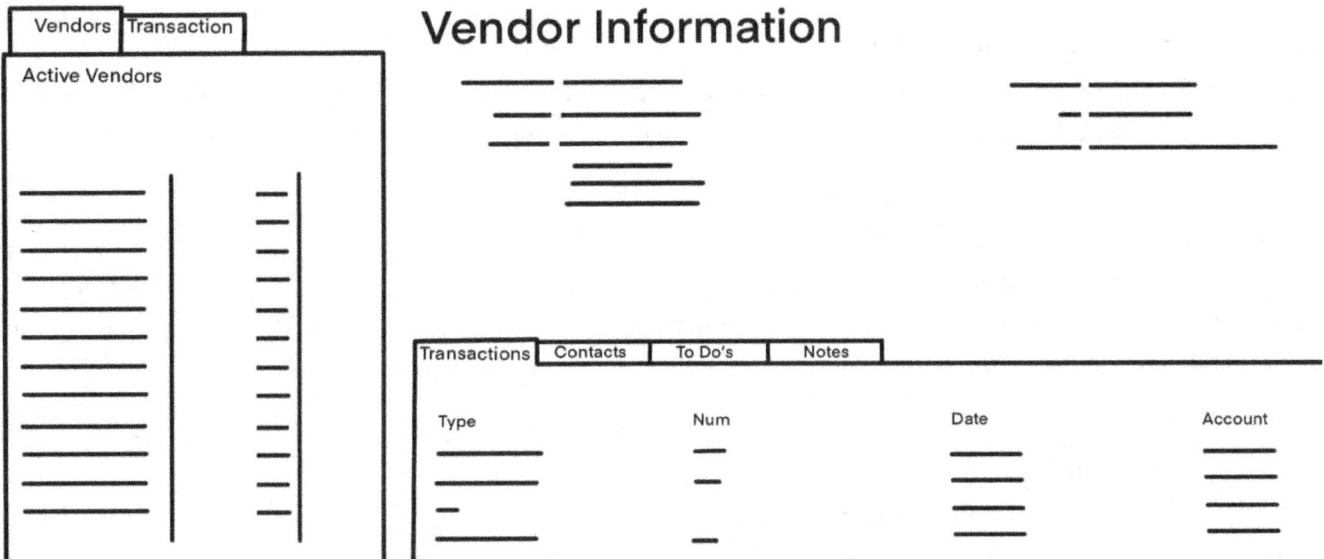

Step 1: Accessing the Vendor Center

To initiate the process of adding vendor information, log in to your QuickBooks Online account. Once logged in, locate and click on the *Vendor Center* tab. The Vendor Center is a dedicated section within QuickBooks Online that allows you to view and manage all your vendor-related activities.

Step 2: Creating a New Vendor Profile

In the Vendor Center, you will find an option to *Add New Vendor* or *Create Vendor*. Click on this option to begin creating a new vendor profile.

Step 3: Entering Vendor Details

A new window will open, prompting you to enter the necessary details of the vendor. Ensure that you provide accurate information such as the vendor's name, contact information, address, phone number, email, and payment terms. Additionally, you may also input a vendor tax ID for tax reporting purposes.

Step 4: Customizing Vendor Settings

QuickBooks Online allows you to customize vendor settings to suit your business requirements. You can set default payment terms and preferred delivery methods and add any specific notes or comments relevant to the vendor.

Step 5: Saving Vendor Information

After filling in the required details and making any necessary customizations, click on the *Save* or *Save and Close* button to store the vendor information in your QuickBooks Online account.

Managing Vendor Information

Adding vendor information is just the first step; effective vendor management requires ongoing maintenance and organization. QuickBooks Online offers several tools to help you manage your vendors efficiently.

Step 1: Viewing Vendor List

To access the list of all your vendors, return to the Vendor Center. Here, you will find a comprehensive list of all the vendors you have added to the system, along with their contact details.

Step 2: Editing Vendor Information

In case of any changes to a vendor's details, click on the vendor's name from the list to open their profile. Then, click on the *Edit* button to make the necessary updates. Remember to save the changes once you've made them.

Step 3: Merging Duplicate Vendor Entries

At times, you might inadvertently create duplicate vendor entries. QuickBooks Online allows for easy merging of such duplicate entries. To do this, identify the duplicate vendors, select the relevant entries, and choose the *Merge Vendors* option. The system will guide you through the process of consolidating the information.

Step 4: Vendor Contact History

Maintaining a good relationship with vendors is vital for the smooth functioning of your business. QuickBooks Online enables you to access the contact history of a specific vendor. This feature allows you to view previous interactions, including emails and notes, providing valuable context during future engagements.

Recording and Categorizing Expenses

Accurate expense recording and categorization are essential for budgeting, financial reporting, and tax compliance. QuickBooks Online simplifies this process by offering intuitive expense recording features.

Step 1: Entering Expenses

To record expenses, go to the *Expenses* tab on the QuickBooks Online dashboard. Click on *New Expense* to create a new entry.

Step 2: Selecting Vendor

In the expense form, select the vendor associated with the expense from the dropdown menu. If the vendor is not yet added to the system, you can create a new vendor profile directly from the expense form.

Step 3: Expense Details

Provide the necessary details of the expense, such as the expense date, payment method, and description. Additionally, assign an appropriate expense category to ensure accurate tracking and reporting.

Step 4: Attaching Receipts

For documentation and compliance purposes, you can attach digital copies of receipts or invoices related to the expense directly within QuickBooks Online.

Step 5: Save and Verify

Double-check all the details entered before clicking on the *Save* or *Save and Close* button to finalize the expense entry.

Step 6: Categorizing Expenses

QuickBooks Online allows you to create customized expense categories that align with your business needs. Proper categorization ensures that expenses are classified accurately and can be analyzed for budgeting and cost management purposes.

Tracking Bills and Managing Payments

Tracking bills and managing payments efficiently is a crucial aspect of financial management for any business. QuickBooks Online provides a user-friendly interface and robust tools to streamline the process of tracking bills, making payments, and maintaining financial transparency. Below is a step-by-step procedure to guide you through the process:

Step 1: Accessing the Vendor Center

1. Launch QuickBooks Online and log in to your account.
2. From the main dashboard, navigate to the *Expenses* tab on the left-hand menu.
3. Click on *Vendors* to access the Vendor Center, where you can view and manage all your vendor-related activities.

Step 2: Entering Bills

1. In the Vendor Center, click the *New Transaction* or + button, then select *Bill* from the drop-down menu.
2. Choose the vendor from the list or add a new vendor by clicking *Add New*.
3. Enter the necessary details of the bill, such as the billing date, due date, and the amount due.
4. Assign the appropriate expense category to the bill to ensure accurate expense tracking and reporting.
5. Optionally, attach any relevant documents, such as invoices or receipts, to the bill entry.
6. Click *Save and close* to record the bill in QuickBooks Online.

Step 3: Setting Bill Payment Reminders

1. To avoid missing due dates, navigate to the *Expenses* tab on the left-hand menu and click on *Vendors*.
2. Find the vendor for whom you want to set up payment reminders and click on their name to open their vendor profile.
3. In the vendor profile, click on the *Edit* button.
4. Under *Payment and billing settings*, check the box that says *Payment reminders*.
5. Configure the reminder settings, such as the number of days before the due date you want to be reminded and choose the email address to which the reminders should be sent.
6. Click *Save* to enable the payment reminders for that vendor.

Step 4: Making Bill Payments

1. To pay a bill, go to the Vendor Center and find the vendor from the list.
2. Click on the vendor's name to view their profile and outstanding bills.
3. Locate the bill you want to pay and click on the *Make payment* button next to it.
4. Enter the payment details, such as the payment method (e.g., check, credit card, bank transfer) and the payment date.
5. If you're paying only a partial amount, specify the amount in the *Amount* field.
6. QuickBooks Online automatically applies the payment to the bill. Ensure that the correct bill is selected for payment.
7. If there are several invoices to settle for a single vendor, you can select them all and pay them in a batch.
8. Click *Save and close* to record the payment and mark the bill as *Paid*.

Step 5: Utilizing Bill Payment Automation (Optional)

QuickBooks Online offers bill payment automation features that can save time and effort. To set up automatic bill payments:

1. Go to the Gear icon in the top right corner and select *Account and Settings*.
2. Click on the *Bills and expenses* tab.
3. Under *Bill automation*, select *Automatically apply credits* and *Automatically mark bills as paid*.
4. Choose the preferred payment account and set up the default payment delay.
5. Click *Save* to enable bill payment automation.

Step 6: Generating Reports

To gain insights into your bill payments and expenses, you can generate various reports in QuickBooks Online.

1. Go to the *Reports* tab on the left-hand menu.
2. Under *Expense and vendors*, explore reports like *Expenses by Vendor Detail*, *Unpaid Bills*, and *Vendor Balance Summary*.
3. Customize the report parameters to fit your specific requirements.
4. Examine the reports to make knowledgeable financial choices and monitor your business cash flow.

By following this step-by-step procedure, you can effectively track bills and manage payments in QuickBooks Online. Utilizing the software's features for vendor management and expense tracking, you can streamline your financial processes, reduce errors, and gain better control over your business's financial health.

How To Access the Payment History of Vendors?

Accessing the payment history of vendors in QuickBooks Online (QBO) allows you to review all payments made to a particular vendor. This can be useful for reconciling accounts, verifying expenses, or simply keeping track of your business's spending patterns with specific vendors. Here's a simple step-by-step guide to help you access the payment history of vendors in QBO:

Step 1: Log in to QuickBooks Online

Step 2: Go to the Vendors Section

1. On the left sidebar, click on *Expenses* or *Vendors* (the exact wording might vary based on your QBO version).
2. This will take you to the vendor center, where you can see a list of all your vendors.

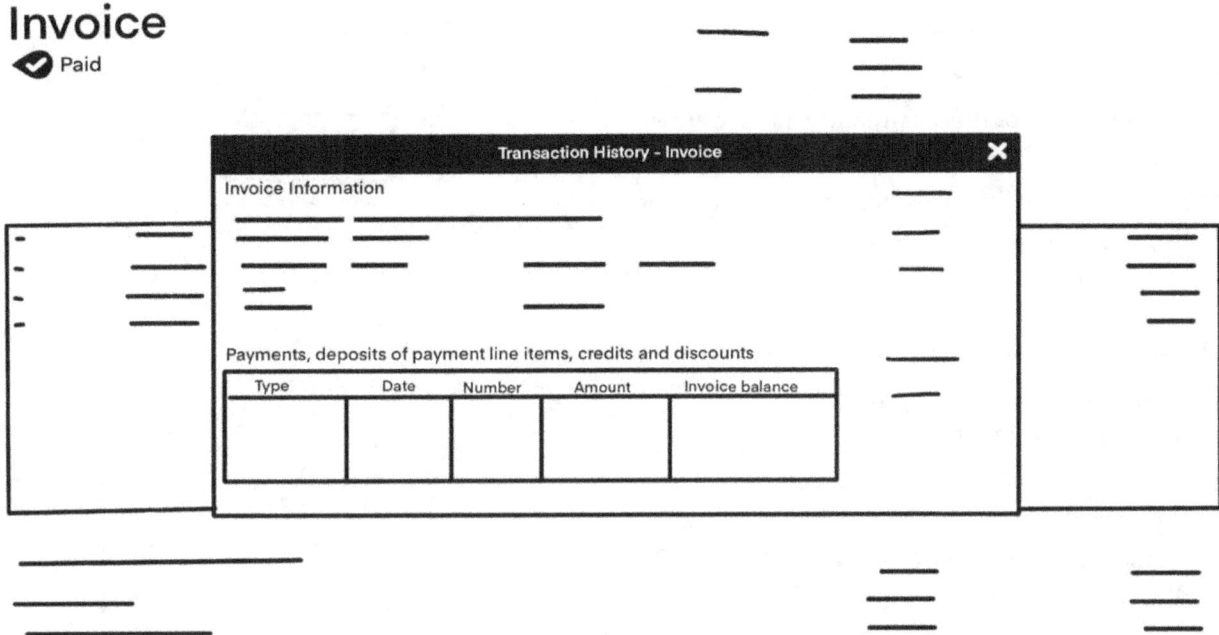

Step 3: Select the Desired Vendor

1. From the list of vendors, click on the vendor whose payment history you want to view.
2. This will open up the vendor's detail page.

Step 4: View Transaction List

1. On the vendor's detail page, you'll see a list of all transactions related to that vendor. This includes bills, payments, and any other related transactions.
2. To specifically view payments, look for transactions labeled as *Payment* or *Bill Payment*.

Step 5: Filter and Sort (If Needed)

1. If you have a long history with the vendor and want to view payments from a specific period, use the filter option. You can set a date range to narrow down the transactions.
2. You can also sort the transactions by date, amount, or type to make it easier to find specific payments.

Step 6: Click on a Payment for Details

1. If you want more details about a particular payment, click on it. This will open a detailed view where you can see the payment date, method, amount, and any associated notes or attachments.

Step 7: Export or Print (Optional)

1. If you need a physical copy or want to save the payment history for your records, you can export the list to Excel or print it directly from QBO.

Quote, Estimates, and Job Costing

Quote & Estimates

A quote or an estimate is a document that provides a potential customer with a breakdown of the expected costs for a particular job or service. It's a way to let the customer know how much a job might cost before any work begins.

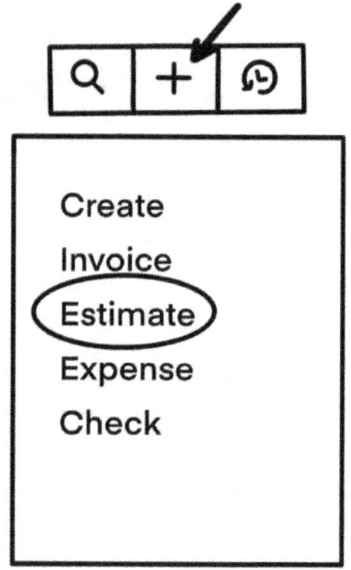

Instructions for Creating an Estimate in QBO

1. Log in to QuickBooks Online.
2. On the left sidebar, click on *+ New*.
3. From the dropdown, select *Estimate.*
4. Choose the customer you're sending the estimate to from the *Customer* dropdown.
5. Fill in the necessary details:
   - Date: The date you're creating the estimate.
   - Expiry Date: The date until which the estimate is valid.
   - Products/Services: The items you'll be providing or the tasks you'll be performing.
   - Rate & Quantity: The cost of each item or task and the quantity.
6. The total amount will be calculated automatically.
7. Add any additional notes or terms if necessary.
8. Click *Save and send* to email the estimate directly to the customer or *Save and close* to save it for later.

Job Costing

Job costing is a method used to determine the cost of a specific job or project. It involves tracking all the costs related to a job to determine its profitability. This includes materials, labor, overheads, and any other expenses.

Instructions for Job Costing in QBO

1. Set Up Customers and Jobs:
   - Go to the Sales or Invoicing tab.

- Click on Customers.
- Add a new customer for each job or project.

2. Track Expenses for Each Job:
   - Whenever you enter a bill, check, or expense, ensure you associate it with the appropriate customer or job.
   - Use the Customer/Project column to allocate each expense to a specific job.

3. Use Products and Services:
   - Set up products or services in QBO for different types of labor or materials.
   - When entering transactions, select the appropriate product or service and assign it to the relevant job.

4. Run Job Costing Reports:
   - Go to Reports.
   - Search for Job Costs or Project Costs.
   - Run the report to see a breakdown of all costs associated with each job.

5. Review and Analyze:
   - Regularly review your job costing reports to determine the profitability of each job.
   - Adjust pricing or reduce costs, if necessary, based on your findings.

Chapter 8
Managing Funds and Deposits

Effectively managing funds and deposits is crucial for any business to maintain accurate financial records and ensure smooth cash flow. In this chapter, we will delve into the concept of undeposited funds and their purpose, as well as explore various aspects of managing funds and deposits in QuickBooks Online.

What are Undeposited Funds and Their Purpose?

Undeposited funds are a crucial component of efficient cash flow management for businesses. When customers make payments for products or services, those funds are typically received in the form of checks, cash, or electronic payments. Rather than depositing each payment into the business's bank account immediately, which can be time-consuming and lead to potential errors, undeposited funds provide a temporary holding account within QuickBooks Online.

Receive Payment

Customer		Amount received
[⌄] [ ]		**$0.00**

Payment date
[ ]

Payment method	Reference no.	Deposit to		Amount received
[⌄]	[ ]	[⌄]		0.00

➕ Add new Undeposi

Undeposited Funds *Other Current Asset*

Memo
[ ]

📎 Attachments
[ ]

The primary purpose of undeposited funds is to streamline the process of depositing multiple payments into the bank at once. As transactions are recorded in QuickBooks Online, the system automatically creates entries in the Undeposited Funds account for each received payment. These funds remain in this virtual holding account until the business owner or bookkeeper is ready to combine and deposit them into the actual bank account as a single lump sum.

By using the Undeposited Funds account, businesses can better organize their cash flow, making it easier to manage and track customer payments. This approach also facilitates smoother bank reconciliations, reducing the likelihood of discrepancies between the company's financial records and the bank statements.

In QuickBooks Online, *Undeposited Funds* is an internal account that acts as a temporary holding place for money that you've received but hasn't yet deposited to the bank. Think of it as a virtual drawer where you keep checks or payments until you take them to the bank.

Imagine you receive multiple checks from customers in a single day but deposit them all together as one lump sum in the bank. Instead of recording each check as a separate deposit in QBO, you can group them together in the Undeposited Funds account. Later, when you make the actual bank deposit, you can match it to the combined total of the checks, ensuring your QBO bank balance aligns with your real-world bank statement.

How Undeposited Funds Work

Receiving Payments:

- When you receive a payment from a customer, go to the *Receive Payment* screen.
- Instead of choosing a bank account for the deposit, select *Undeposited Funds* as the deposit destination.

Grouping Payments:

- Over time, as you receive more payments, they'll accumulate in the Undeposited Funds account.
- These payments stay here until you're ready to deposit them into your bank.

Making a Bank Deposit:

When you're ready to deposit the funds into your bank:

1. Go to the + *New* button and select *Bank Deposit*.
2. You'll see a list of all payments in Undeposited Funds.
3. Select the payments you're depositing together.
4. The total deposit amount in QBO should match the lump sum you're depositing in your real-world bank.
5. Choose the bank account you're depositing to, then *Save and close*.

Reconciliation:

When reconciling your bank account in QBO, the lump sum deposit should match the bank statement, making the reconciliation process smoother.

Benefits of Using the Undeposited Funds Account

Utilizing the Undeposited Funds account in QuickBooks Online offers several advantages that contribute to the overall financial health and efficiency of a business:

- **Organized Deposits:** One of the significant benefits of using the Undeposited Funds account is that it helps maintain a clear and organized record of customer payments. Instead of multiple individual deposits in the bank account, businesses can consolidate payments into a single deposit, simplifying the bank reconciliation process.

- **Reduced Errors:** The process of combining payments into a single deposit significantly reduces the likelihood of errors in the depositing process. Since the deposits in QuickBooks Online correspond directly to the lump sum deposited in the bank, there is less room for discrepancies between the accounting records and the bank statements.
- **Efficient Reconciliation:** Reconciling bank deposits with the corresponding bank statements becomes more straightforward when undeposited funds are utilized. The deposit recorded in QuickBooks Online can be matched against the actual deposit made into the bank account, ensuring that all transactions are accurately recorded and accounted for.
- **Improved Cash Flow Management:** By holding customer payments in the Undeposited Funds account until they are deposited as a lump sum, businesses can gain better control over their cash flow. They can strategically choose when to make bank deposits, aligning them with their financial needs and optimizing fund availability.
- **Enhanced Financial Reporting:** Utilizing the Undeposited Funds account provides a more accurate picture of the business's current financial position. The account helps capture pending deposits, ensuring that the balance sheet and income statements reflect the true financial status of the company.

Managing Undeposited Funds Effectively

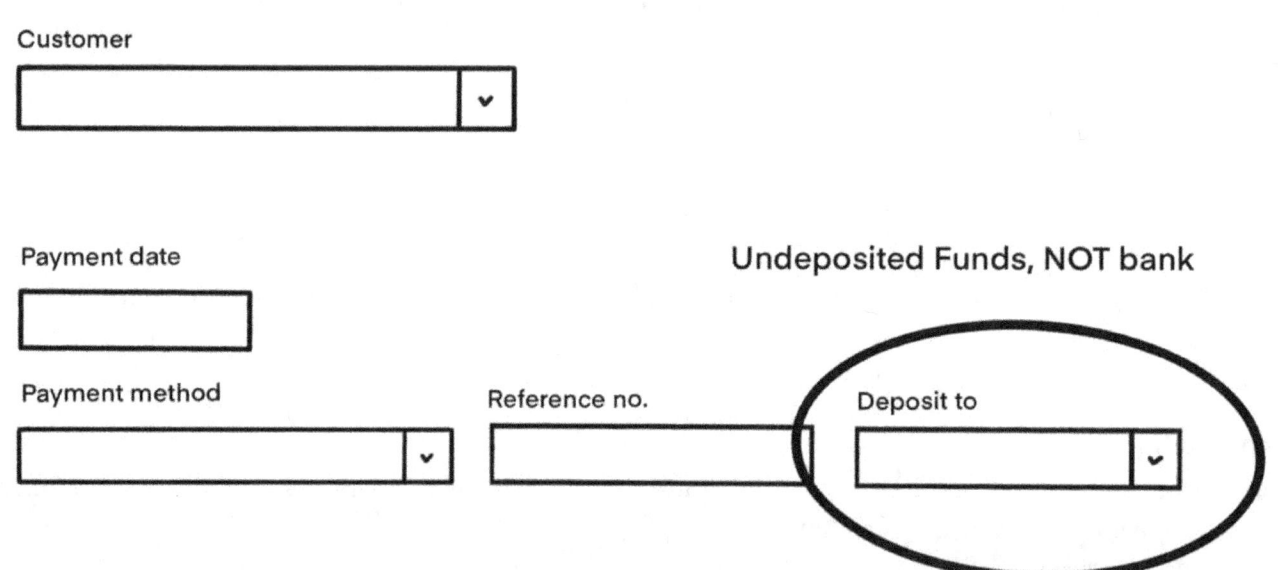

Effective management of undeposited funds is integral to maintaining accurate financial records and streamlining the deposit process in QuickBooks Online. By understanding the purpose of undeposited funds and following the correct procedures for creating deposits, linking payments, reconciling bank deposits, and troubleshooting errors, businesses can enhance their financial management practices.

Regular audits further contribute to deposit accuracy, ensuring that any discrepancies are promptly identified and resolved. With a thorough grasp of managing undeposited funds, companies can strengthen their financial management processes, make informed decisions, and foster financial stability and growth.

Creating a New Deposit in QuickBooks Online

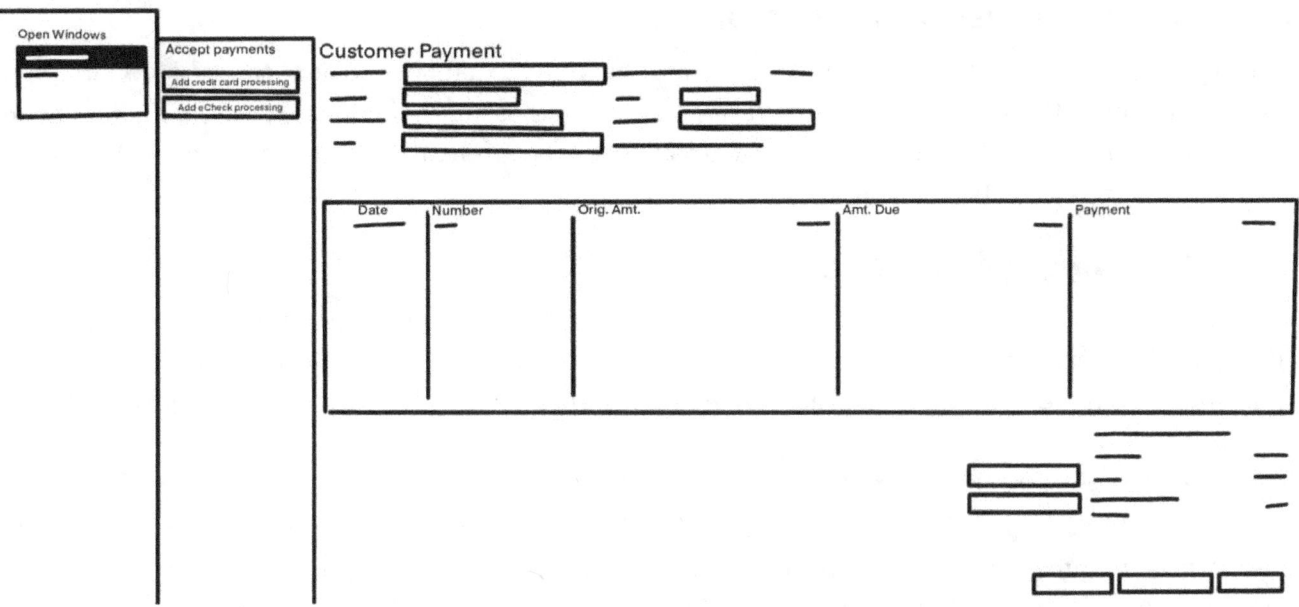

Now that we have a comprehensive understanding of undeposited funds and their significance let us walk through the step-by-step process of creating a new deposit in QuickBooks Online:

Step 1: Accessing the Deposit Feature

To begin the process, log in to your QuickBooks Online account and navigate to the home page. From the main dashboard, locate and click on the *Plus (+)* icon, which will reveal a drop-down menu. From this menu, select *Bank Deposit* under the *Other* section.

Step 2: Selecting the Deposit Account

Once you have accessed the *Bank Deposit* window, the next crucial step is to choose the appropriate bank account into which the funds will be deposited. From the *Account* drop-down menu, select the desired bank account that corresponds to the physical deposit you are about to make.

Step 3: Reviewing the Payments After selecting the bank account,

QuickBooks Online will display a list of payments available in the *Select the payments included in this deposit* section. Carefully review and ensure that all the payments you intend to include in this deposit are listed. If any payment is missing, you might need to reconcile undeposited funds or investigate further to identify any potential discrepancies.

Step 4: Allocating Payments

Once you have reviewed the payments and confirmed their accuracy, it is time to allocate them to the appropriate accounts. QuickBooks Online allows you to categorize payments into different accounts, such as revenue accounts or specific income categories. This step ensures that the deposit is recorded accurately in the general ledger and aligns with the corresponding financial transactions.

Step 5: Handling Fees and Adjustments

In some cases, you might encounter additional fees or adjustments that need to be accounted for within the deposit. QuickBooks Online provides the flexibility to include these fees and make necessary adjustments to the deposit amount. This feature helps in maintaining a comprehensive and precise financial record, reflecting the true value of the deposit.

Step 6: Verifying Information

Before finalizing the deposit, it is crucial to double-check all the information entered during the process. Verify the deposit amount, the allocated accounts, and any adjustments made. Taking a few moments to review the data ensures accuracy and prevents potential errors that might affect future financial analysis.

Step 7: Saving and Recording the Deposit

Once you are confident that all the information is accurate, click on the *Save and Close* button to record the deposit officially. QuickBooks Online will then update the selected bank account with the new deposit amount, and the transactions will be reflected in the corresponding accounts within the general ledger.

Linking Customer Payments to Deposits

One of the key advantages of using undeposited funds is the ability to link customer payments to their respective deposits accurately. This linkage is crucial for proper revenue recognition, as it allows businesses to track which payments have been included in specific bank deposits.

To link customer payments to deposits in QuickBooks Online, follow these steps:

Step 1: Accessing Customer Payments

From the main dashboard in QuickBooks Online, click on the *Sales* tab in the left-hand menu and select *Customers* from the drop-down menu. Find and select the customer whose payment you want to associate with a deposit.

Step 2: Applying Payment to an Invoice

Within the customer's profile, you will find a list of transactions related to that customer. Locate the payment you want to link to a deposit and click on it to open the transaction details. In this section, you can apply the payment to the corresponding invoice(s) and specify the deposit to which the payment belongs.

Step 3: Selecting the Deposit

Upon applying the payment to the invoice(s), click on the *Deposit to* drop-down menu. From the options presented, choose *Undeposited Funds* to indicate that the payment will be included in the next deposit. Alternatively, if the payment was received and deposited in the bank immediately, you can select the specific bank account to which the payment was deposited.

Step 4: Saving the Transaction

After selecting the appropriate deposit, click on the *Save and close* button to finalize the linkage between the customer payment and the deposit. QuickBooks Online will now reflect this information in the respective accounts, ensuring accurate revenue recognition and deposit management.

Handling Partial Payments and Overpayments

In the dynamic world of business transactions, it is not uncommon for customers to make partial payments toward their invoices or purchases. Managing these partial payments accurately is vital for maintaining clear and accurate financial records. QuickBooks Online offers a straightforward procedure to handle such situations efficiently.

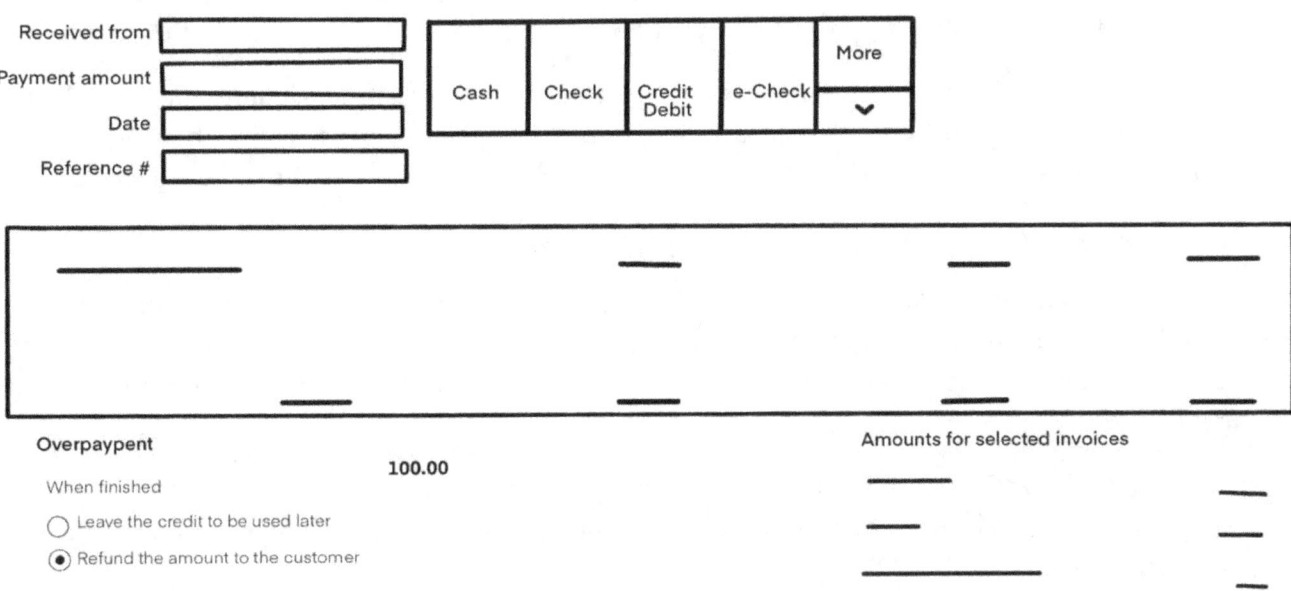

Partial Payments

- **Recording Partial Payments:** When a customer submits a partial payment, the first step is to record the transaction accurately. To do this, navigate to the *Sales* menu and select *Customers*. Locate the customer who made the partial payment and click on their name to open the customer profile. Next, select the open invoice related to the payment and click *Receive Payment.* Enter the amount of the partial payment received and ensure that the payment date is correct. QuickBooks Online will automatically update the remaining balance on the invoice.

- **Tracking Partial Payments:** QuickBooks Online provides an easy way to track all partial payments made by customers. By generating a customer payment report, businesses can have a comprehensive overview of the payments received, outstanding balances, and any past partial payments made.

Managing Overpayments

Occasionally, customers might unintentionally overpay their invoices or accounts, leading to an excess of funds in the Undeposited Funds account. Dealing with overpayments efficiently is essential to maintain the accuracy of the financial records and provide exceptional customer service. Here's how to handle overpayments in QuickBooks Online.

1. Identifying Overpayments: To identify overpayments, businesses must regularly review their Undeposited Funds account. QuickBooks Online allows users to generate reports that list all transactions held in the Undeposited Funds account, making it easier to spot overpayments.

2. Creating Credit Memos or Refunds: Once an overpayment is identified, businesses have two primary options: they can either issue a credit memo or process a refund to the customer. If the customer is likely to make future purchases, a credit memo can be applied to their account, effectively reducing their outstanding balance. On the other hand, if the customer prefers a refund, the business can process it directly from the *Sales Receipt* window by selecting *Refund the Amount to the Customer*.

3. Applying Credit Memos or Refunds: After creating credit memos or refunds, they need to be appropriately applied to future transactions or issued as a check. This ensures that the overpaid amount is adequately accounted for, and the customer's account reflects the correct balance.

Reconciling Bank Deposits with Bank Statements

Reconciling bank deposits involves comparing the deposits recorded in QuickBooks Online with the corresponding entries on the bank statement. This procedure aids in detecting any inconsistencies or mistakes, guaranteeing that the financial records are a true representation of the actual banking transactions.

1. Access the *Banking* tab in QuickBooks Online and select *Reconcile*.
2. Identify the bank account you want to reconcile and input the date and final balance from the bank statement.
3. QuickBooks Online will display a list of all deposits and payments within the specified period.
4. Match the deposits on the bank statement with the corresponding entries in QuickBooks Online.
5. Mark each matched deposit as *Cleared* by clicking on the checkbox next to it.
6. If there are any deposits on the bank statement that are not in QuickBooks Online, add them as *Deposits in Transit*.
7. Similarly, if there are any deposits in QuickBooks Online that do not appear on the bank statement, add them as *Outstanding Deposits*.

8. Account for any bank fees, interest, or other adjustments to ensure the ending balance in QuickBooks Online matches the ending balance on the bank statement.

9. Once all entries are reconciled, click *Finish Now* to complete the reconciliation process.

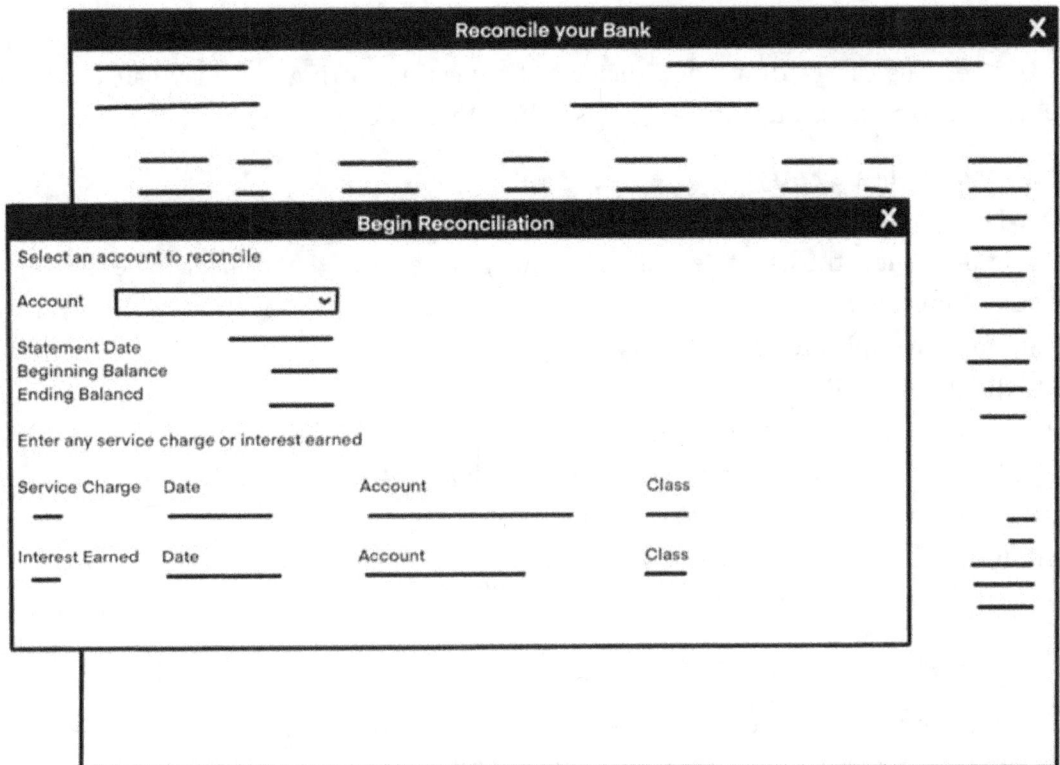

Identifying and Resolving Deposit Discrepancies

Sometimes, the deposit amount for an invoice payment in your QuickBooks Online banking transactions may differ from the outstanding balance due to various factors, such as bank processing times or manual entry errors. How do you reconcile the deposit with the bill and log the client payment? Be sure to match the bank feed amount, pay the invoice, and avoid adding a new sale to your books. It may be pretty perplexing!

1. After recognizing the payment in your bank feed:
2. Click *Find Match* to find the bill we should apply the payment to:
3. After that, you choose the invoice to which you want to record the payment:
4. Enter the entire invoice amount on the right side, then scroll down to make up the difference:
5. Add the difference to the area for resolving transactions.

Remember: You might wish to accept only partial payment of the invoice and follow up for the balance due from your client if your customer should have paid in full or you weren't expecting fees to be deducted.

This strategy works well when your bank deducts money from your customer's payment or when credit card fees, such as stripe fees, are deducted.

Dealing with Duplicate or Missing Deposits

Duplicate Deposits

Duplicate deposits can arise when a user unintentionally records the same deposit entry multiple times in QuickBooks Online. This can lead to inaccuracies in financial reporting and may cause confusion during bank reconciliation. To address duplicate deposits, follow these steps:

1. Identify the Duplicate Entry:
   - Navigate to the *Deposits* section in QuickBooks Online.
   - Carefully review the list of deposits to identify any entries that appear to be duplicated.
2. Open the Duplicate Deposit:
   - Click on the duplicate deposit entry to open the details.
3. Delete the Duplicate Entry:
   - In the deposit, details view, click on the *More* option and select *Delete*.
   - Confirm the deletion to remove the duplicate deposit from the system.
4. Verify Changes:
   - After deleting the duplicate entry, ensure that the deposit total and related customer payments reflect the correct information.

Missing Deposits

Missing deposits occur when payments received from customers are not properly recorded as deposits in QuickBooks Online. Failure to record all deposits can lead to discrepancies between the company's financial records and bank statements. To address missing deposits, follow these steps:

1. Cross-Check with Bank Statements:
   - Retrieve the relevant bank statements for the period in question.
   - Compare the deposits listed in QuickBooks Online with the corresponding deposits on the bank statements.
2. Identify Missing Deposits:
   - Note any deposits that appear on the bank statements but are not recorded in QuickBooks Online.
3. Create a New Deposit Entry:
   - Once missing deposits are identified, create new deposit entries in QuickBooks Online for each one.
4. Verify Customer Payments:
   - Ensure that the new deposit entries accurately reflect the total amount deposited and link them to the appropriate customer payments.

Cleanup Undeposited Funds Workflow

Cleaning up undeposited funds in QuickBooks Online involves several steps to ensure that all payments are accurately deposited and recorded.

Bank and Credit Cards | Checking

Checking		Savings	
$-3,621.93 Bank balance **$1,456.00** In Quickbooks	**23**	**$200.00** Bank balance **$800.00** In Quickbooks	**1**

For Review | In Quickbooks | Excluded

Step 1: Review Undeposited Funds Register

To initiate the cleanup process, access the Undeposited Funds Register in QuickBooks Online. This register acts as a holding place for all received payments that haven't been deposited yet. Review the register carefully to identify any discrepancies or duplicate entries that may have occurred due to manual errors or system glitches.

Step 2: Match Payments with Invoices

The next step is to match the payments listed in the Undeposited Funds Register with their corresponding invoices or sales receipts. QuickBooks Online provides tools to reconcile payments automatically with open invoices, making the process more efficient and reducing the chances of overlooking any transactions.

Step 3: Create Group Deposits

Once all payments are accurately matched with their respective invoices, you can proceed to create group deposits. In this step, you select the payments that belong to a single bank deposit and combine them into a single entry. This consolidation mirrors how these payments will appear on your actual bank statement.

Step 4: Bank Deposit Entry

Now, it's time to create a bank deposit entry in QuickBooks Online. Enter the combined amount from the group deposit and select the appropriate bank account where the actual deposit will be made. Cross-verify the deposit date and other relevant details to ensure accuracy.

Step 5: Reconcile Bank Deposits

After creating the bank deposit entry, it's essential to reconcile it with the actual deposit made to your bank account. QuickBooks Online provides reconciliation tools that allow you to match the deposits in the software with the deposits in your bank statement. This step helps identify any discrepancies and ensures that all transactions are accounted for correctly.

Step 6: Verify Deposit Accuracy

To maintain accurate financial records, it's essential to verify the deposit accuracy regularly. Perform regular audits to cross-check the bank deposits in QuickBooks Online with the corresponding bank statements. Address any discrepancies promptly to avoid potential accounting errors.

Troubleshooting Common Errors in Deposit Recording

In the dynamic world of accounting, even with the user-friendly nature of QuickBooks Online, errors can still occur during the deposit recording process. Such errors can lead to discrepancies in financial reports, hamper decision-making, and create confusion during the reconciliation process. It is essential for businesses to identify and resolve these errors promptly to ensure the accuracy and integrity of their financial data. This section will delve into the most common errors encountered during deposit recording in QuickBooks Online and provide comprehensive troubleshooting steps to rectify them effectively.

Duplicate Deposits

One of the most frequent errors users may encounter is duplicate deposits. Duplicate deposits occur when the same transaction is recorded multiple times, leading to overstated income and erroneous financial reports. This can happen due to various reasons, such as accidental double entries or system glitches. Resolving duplicate deposits is crucial to maintain accurate financial records and prevent skewed data.

To troubleshoot duplicate deposits, follow these steps:

1. **Identify Duplicate Entries:** Begin by running a thorough review of the deposit records in QuickBooks Online. Look for transactions with identical dates, amounts, and payment details. Pay attention to deposits recorded for the same customer or source of income on the same day.
2. **Cross-Check Source Documents:** After identifying potential duplicates, cross-check them with the source documents, such as bank statements and customer receipts. This step helps verify if the deposits indeed occurred more than once or if there are any discrepancies between QuickBooks Online and actual transactions.
3. **Delete Duplicate Deposits:** Once confirmed, proceed to delete the duplicate deposits from QuickBooks Online. To do this, open the deposit transaction, select the *More* option, and click on *Delete*. QuickBooks Online will prompt a confirmation message before permanently removing the duplicate entry.
4. **Conduct Regular Data Audits:** To prevent future occurrences of duplicate deposits, implement regular data audits. These audits should be performed at regular intervals, such as monthly or quarterly, to ensure the accuracy of recorded transactions and promptly address any duplicates that may arise.

Incorrect Payment Allocations

Incorrect payment allocations can lead to discrepancies in deposit records, as funds may be allocated to the wrong customer invoices or sales transactions. This can create confusion during the reconciliation process and make it challenging to track actual payments received from customers. Identifying and rectifying incorrect payment allocations is crucial for maintaining accurate deposit records and financial reporting.

To troubleshoot incorrect payment allocations, follow these steps:

1. **Review Payment Allocation:** Start by reviewing the payment allocations in QuickBooks Online. Ensure that each payment is appropriately allocated to the corresponding customer invoices or sales transactions.
2. **Re-allocate Funds:** If you find any misallocations, proceed to re-allocate the funds correctly. To do this, open the deposit transaction, click on the incorrect allocation, and select *Remove*. Then, reselect the appropriate invoice or transaction from the list of outstanding payments and click *Add*.
3. **Verify Data Entry Accuracy:** Double-check the accuracy of data entry when recording customer payments. Ensure that you are selecting the correct invoices or sales transactions while creating deposits.
4. **Train Staff:** If multiple individuals handle deposit recording, consider providing additional training to ensure consistent and accurate payment allocations. Having a standardized process can significantly reduce the likelihood of allocation errors.

Reconciliation Discrepancies

Reconciliation discrepancies occur when the bank deposits recorded in QuickBooks Online do not match the actual deposits reflected in bank statements. These discrepancies can arise due to timing differences, bank fees, or missed transactions, and they can pose significant challenges during the reconciliation process.

To troubleshoot reconciliation discrepancies, follow these steps:

1. **Review Bank Statements:** Obtain the most recent bank statements and compare the recorded deposits in QuickBooks Online with the actual deposits listed in the statements. Check for any discrepancies in dates, amounts, or payment sources.
2. **Investigate Timing Differences:** Timing differences may occur if deposits made close to the end of a reporting period are not reflected in the bank statement for that period. Ensure that all deposits made within the reporting period are recorded accurately in QuickBooks Online.
3. **Account for Bank Fees:** Sometimes, bank fees or charges may be deducted from the deposits, resulting in differences between the recorded amounts in QuickBooks Online and the bank statements. Take these fees into account during reconciliation.
4. **Locate Missing Transactions:** If there are missing transactions in QuickBooks Online that appear on the bank statements, add them to the system. Ensure that all deposits are properly recorded, even if they were not initially captured in the software.
5. **Utilize Reconciliation Reports:** QuickBooks Online offers reconciliation reports that can help identify discrepancies and provide a clear overview of the discrepancies. Utilize these reports to pinpoint and address any inconsistencies effectively.

Performing Regular Audits to Maintain Deposit Accuracy

While the steps outlined above are essential for managing funds and deposits in QuickBooks Online, performing regular audits is the cornerstone of maintaining deposit accuracy. Regular audits help businesses identify discrepancies, errors, and potential fraud, thereby ensuring the integrity of financial data. By conducting audits at predetermined intervals, businesses can gain confidence in their financial records, make informed decisions, and comply with regulatory requirements.

Here's a comprehensive procedure for conducting regular audits:

Step 1: Establish an Audit Schedule

The first step in performing regular audits for deposit accuracy is to establish an audit schedule. The frequency of audits may vary depending on the size and complexity of the business, industry regulations, and internal policies. Generally, businesses opt for monthly, quarterly, or annual audits. It is crucial to be consistent with the chosen schedule to maintain an ongoing and systematic approach to auditing.

Step 2: Gather Relevant Documentation

Before commencing the audit, gather all relevant financial documentation. This includes bank statements for the audit period, deposit records from QuickBooks Online, and any additional supporting documents. These documents serve as the foundation for the audit, allowing auditors to compare and verify the accuracy of the recorded deposits.

Step 3: Reconcile Deposits

The next step in the audit process is to reconcile the deposits recorded in QuickBooks Online with the corresponding bank statements. This reconciliation ensures that the total deposit amounts match the accounting records and the actual bank transactions. To begin the reconciliation process, follow these sub-steps:

1. **Starting Point:** Begin by comparing the ending balances of the previous audit with the beginning balances of the current audit. This ensures continuity and accuracy in the reconciliation process.
2. **Match Transactions:** Go through each deposit recorded in QuickBooks Online and cross-reference it with the corresponding deposit in the bank statement. Tick off the deposits that match to indicate their reconciliation.
3. **Investigate Discrepancies:** If any discrepancies are found between the QuickBooks Online records and the bank statement, investigate the reasons behind them. Common causes of discrepancies include timing differences, data entry errors, and bank processing delays.

Step 4: Review Deposit Details

Once the reconciliation is complete, conduct a thorough review of the details for each deposit. Pay close attention to the individual payments included in each deposit, ensuring their accuracy and appropriateness. Verify that customer payments are correctly linked to their respective deposits to prevent misallocation of funds.

Step 5: Investigate Discrepancies

During the review process, if you identify any discrepancies or irregularities in the deposit details, it is essential to conduct a comprehensive investigation. Investigating discrepancies is crucial to understanding the root causes of the errors and implementing corrective measures to prevent future occurrences. Reach out to the relevant stakeholders, such as the finance team or customer support, to gather additional information and clarify any uncertainties.

Step 6: Implement Corrective Actions

Based on the findings of the audit and investigation, implement appropriate corrective actions to rectify any errors and improve deposit accuracy. Depending on the nature of the discrepancies, corrective actions may include adjusting deposit amounts, correcting data entry errors, or enhancing internal controls to prevent future errors.

Step 7: Document the Audit Process

Throughout the audit, maintain detailed documentation of the process, including the steps taken, findings, and actions taken to address discrepancies. Proper documentation not only ensures transparency and accountability but also serves as a valuable reference for future audits.

Step 8: Analyze Trends and Patterns

An essential aspect of regular audits is to identify trends and patterns in deposit accuracy over time. Analyzing historical audit data can help businesses understand recurring issues and take proactive measures to prevent them. Additionally, trend analysis can provide insights into the overall financial health of the company, aiding in strategic decision-making.

Step 9: Report and Communicate

After completing the audit, compile a comprehensive report summarizing the audit findings, actions taken, and recommendations for improvement. The report should be communicated to relevant stakeholders, including management, the finance team, and any external auditors or regulatory bodies.

Step 10: Continuous Improvement

The final step in performing regular audits for deposit accuracy is to emphasize continuous improvement. Use the insights gained from the audit process to refine internal processes, strengthen controls, and enhance the overall financial management practices. Embracing a culture of continuous improvement ensures that the company's financial records remain accurate and reliable in the long run.

Chapter 9

Financial Reporting and Analysis

I n the dynamic world of business, financial reporting and analysis play a pivotal role in providing essential insights into the health and performance of a company. It is through these reports that key stakeholders, such as investors, creditors, management, and regulators, can make informed decisions. In this chapter, we delve into the intricacies of financial reporting and analysis, exploring how businesses generate crucial financial reports, analyze their performance, budget, and forecast, and ensure the accuracy of their financial data through the process of closing periods.

Generating Essential Financial Reports

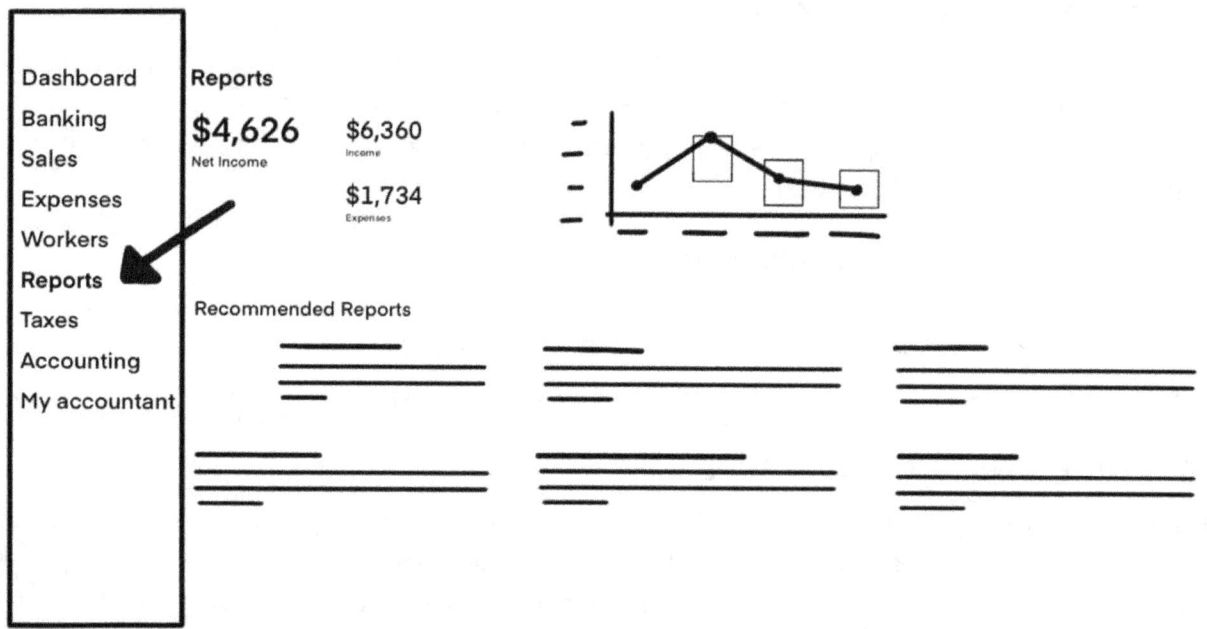

Generating essential financial reports is a fundamental aspect of QuickBooks Online (QBO) that provides businesses with insights into their financial health. Here's a detailed procedure on how to generate these reports:

1. Log in to QuickBooks Online:
    *   Start by signing into your QBO account.
2. Navigate to the Reports Dashboard:

- On the left sidebar, click on *Reports*. This will take you to the main reports dashboard, where you can access a variety of financial reports.

3. Choose the Desired Report: There are several essential financial reports available in QBO. Here are some of the most commonly used:

   - Profit and Loss (P&L) Statement: This shows your income, expenses, and profitability over a specific period.
   - Balance Sheet: Provides a snapshot of your company's assets, liabilities, and equity at a particular point in time.
   - Cash Flow Statement: Displays how changes in balance sheet accounts and income affect cash and cash equivalents.
   - Accounts Receivable Aging: Shows outstanding invoices categorized by the length of time they've been unpaid.
   - Accounts Payable Aging: Displays your outstanding bills categorized by how long they've been due.
   - To generate a report, click on its name from the list or use the search bar at the top to find it.

4. Customize the Report:

   - Date Range: At the top of the report screen, select the desired date range from the dropdown or set a custom range.
   - Filtering: Click on the *Customize* button to access more advanced customization options. Here, you can filter the report by specific customers, vendors, products, services, and more.
   - Display Options: Adjust how the data is presented, such as changing columns, sorting order, or adding subtotals.

5. Run the Report:

   - After setting your desired parameters, click *Run report* to generate the updated version.

6. Review the Report:

   - Carefully review the data presented in the report. Ensure that all transactions appear correctly and that the report aligns with your expectations.

7. Save Customizations (Optional):

   - If you've made specific customizations that you'll use frequently, click on *Save customization* at the top. Give the customized report a name and, if desired, share it with other users in your QBO account.

8. Export the Report:

   - If you need to analyze the data outside of QBO or share it with others, you can export the report.
   - Click on the *Export* icon (usually represented as a sheet with an arrow) at the top of the report.
   - Choose to export as a PDF (for viewing) or as an Excel file (for further data analysis).

9. Schedule Regular Reports (Optional):

   - For reports you need regularly, like monthly financial statements, use the *Schedule* feature. This allows QBO to automatically generate and email the report to specified recipients at set intervals.

10. Return and Explore Other Reports:

   - Go back to the main reports dashboard to explore and generate other essential financial reports as needed.

Analyzing Business Performance

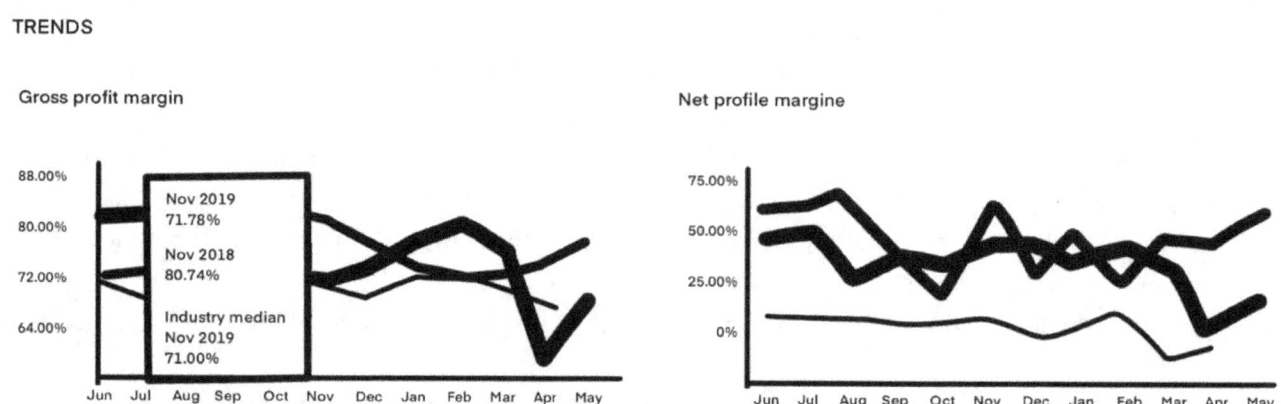

Business performance automatically generates measurements, calculates crucial ratios, and visualizes your client's financial performance. In QuickBooks, formulas and charts are automatically generated for you, providing you with the vital information you need to conduct more persuasive conversations with your clients that will help them expand and increase their profitability.

What the new Business performance tool enables you to achieve is more significant than what it can do. To create a baseline, you might start by looking at past measurements and trends. Then, using industry benchmarks, you may focus on and enhance your customers' business outcomes by comparing your clients' gross and net profit margins to those of similar companies in their industry that are located in the same area and have comparable revenue. Together, you may create goals for your client and check in with them on a regular basis to evaluate how they're doing. You can also compare their performance to that of their colleagues throughout the same period.

The Key Metrics section lists the following five key performance indicators that any company should monitor to increase profitability:

- Income
- Selling prices for products
- Costs of gross profit
- Net income

Eight visual graphs are included in the Trends section and show how several important metrics and ratios have changed over time. These graphs include:

- Margin of gross profit
- Net income margin
- Income Expenses
- Days when payments are due
- Days that are due to be paid
- Present ratio
- Rapid ratio

Each graph includes a link to the underlying report containing the data used for each computation, as well as monthly data from the preceding 12 months compared to the year prior. The charts' clarity makes it simple to visualize a company's business cycle and spot areas for expansion and investment. The updated overview also shows when a business would need to control its spending and make financial sacrifices to get through tougher months.

Business performance equips you with the skills you need to step up your game and boost client prosperity through your knowledge and direction.

Where Can I Locate It?

The Overview tab will show up at the top of the sidebar menu when you log into a client's business using QuickBooks Online Accountant. Select *Business performance* from the secondary menu by hovering your cursor above the tab.

Menu > Overview > Financial Results

As an alternative, you can visit the dashboard by going to the Overview page's main page and selecting the Business Performance tab. All of the QuickBooks Online Simple Start, Essentials, and Plus clients on your client list will have Business Performance. Business Performance is also now available for your own company! You can find it in QuickBooks Online Accountant's Your Books section under the Overview tab (industry benchmarks are not yet available for your particular company).

What Is Its Use?

Business performance is the ideal place to begin when analyzing previous performance and setting new objectives during client meetings. Spend some time investigating and determining which growth comparisons and KPIs are most crucial for your client. You can proceed through each part by following the procedures below, but you can also skip ahead to the metric(s) that are most important to you, depending on your desired objectives.

Step 1: View Important Metrics
1. Obtain a high-level picture of the financial and business growth health.
2. TIP: The circle will be green if a metric's growth has improved in comparison to the prior time period. The circle will turn orange in the event that it has declined.

Step 2: Comparing growth periods
1. Performance should be compared to the prior month, quarter, and year. To choose the time period and comparison, use the two dropdowns on the right. The options provided in the *Compare to* option may change depending on the *Current Period* choice.

Step 3: Monitor Emerging Trends
1. Utilize trends to determine how your client's metrics have evolved over the last year. You may quickly see patterns and learn more about the company using the charts.
2. Select the Previous year above each graphic to compare the data for the current year to those from the year prior. Comparing your client's performance to that of others in the same industry is step 3.1.

Important: If you intend to build the budget from scratch, you don't need to follow these procedures.

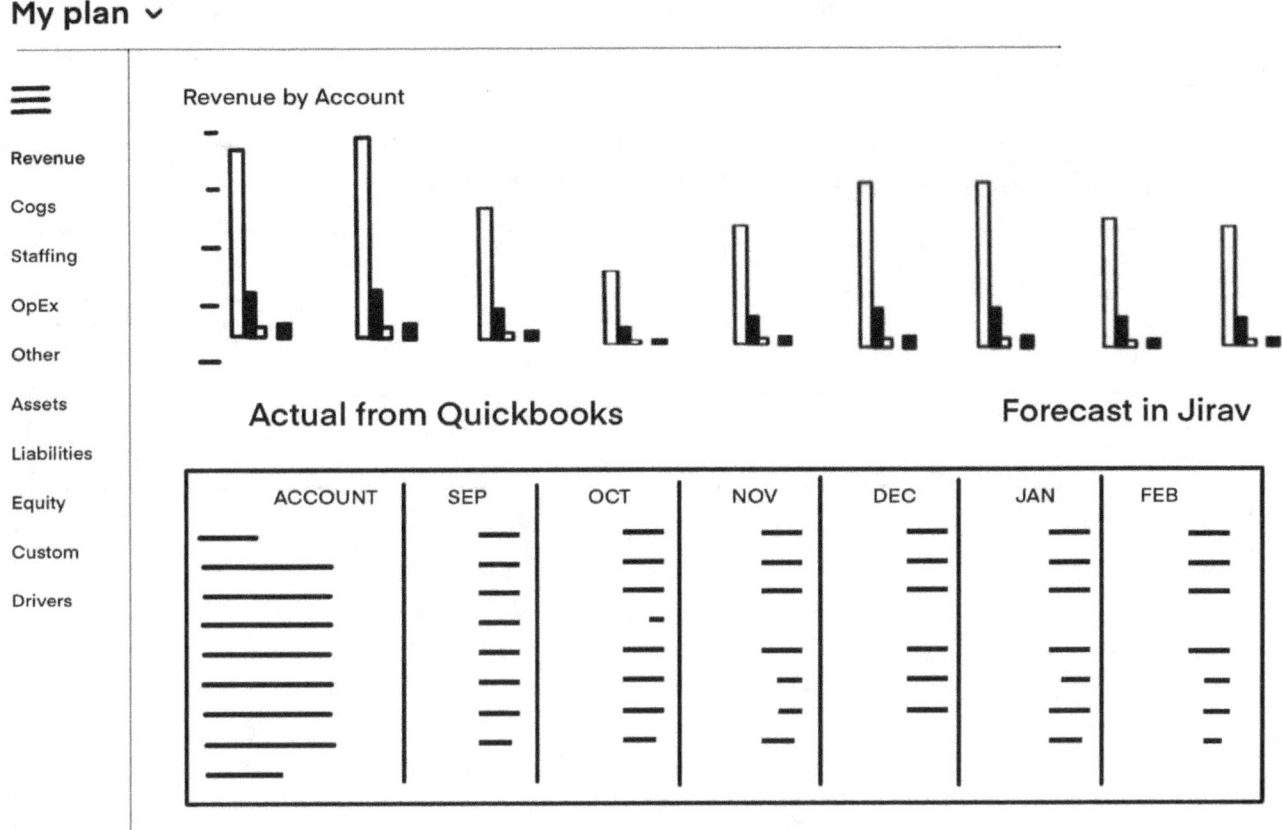

How Can a Budget Be Created in QuickBooks Desktop?

The steps for setting up a budget using QuickBooks Desktop are listed below. Keep up with them step by step.

1. Go to the *Company* menu in QuickBooks after it is open.
2. Select the *Create New Budget* option after clicking *Set Up Budgets* under *Planning and Budgeting*.
3. Select the budget's fiscal year, then either *Profit and Loss* or *Balance Sheet*.
4. If you select *Profit and Loss*, you have also the option to include extra parameters like *Jobs* or *Class Tracking*.
5. After clicking *Next*, choose either *Create Budget from Scratch* or *Create Budget from the Actual Data from the Prior Year,* keeping in mind that you selected *Profit and Loss*.
6. Click *Finish* when you're finished.

Important: If you rename the account after setting the budget, the budget will no longer be associated with that account. Define a new budget for it if you decide to undertake it.

How May a Forecast Be Made in QuickBooks Desktop?

To generate a financial forecast in your QuickBooks Desktop program, adhere to the instructions provided.

1. Open QuickBooks Desktop and select *Company* Menu from the menu.
2. Select *Create New Forecast* after clicking *Set Up Forecast* under *Planning and Budgeting*.

3. Select the forecasting fiscal year.
4. You can also choose to include optional criteria like *Job tracking* or *Class tracking*.
5. Either *Create Forecast from Scratch* or *Create Forecast using Last Year's Actual Data* should be selected.
6. Finally, click *Finish*.

Customizing Reports to Meet Your Needs

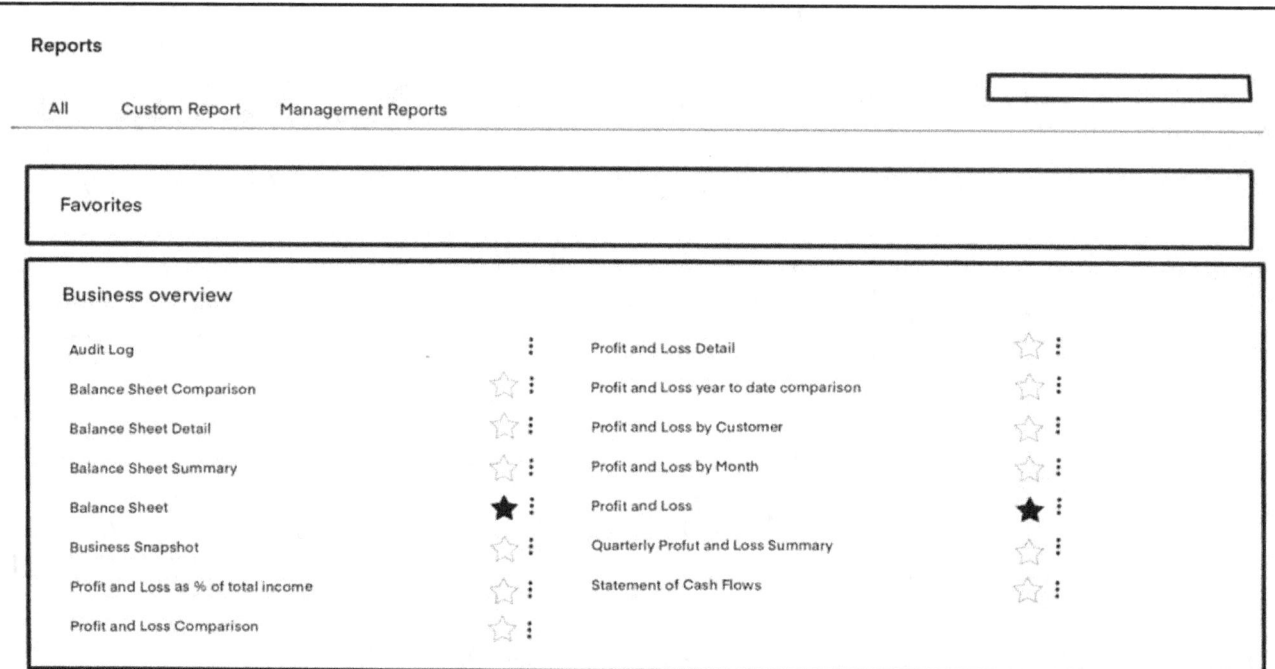

Any firm needs financial reports since they give them insight into the company's performance and cash flow. The highly structured and organized QuickBooks Custom Reports offer valuable business insights from Raw Data. Everyone has various business needs, so you might also want to tailor your reports to reflect the things that are most important to you. Let's look at the simple methods for creating custom reports:

1. On the left-hand menu, select *Reports*.
2. Decide which Report you want to read.
3. Click the *Customize* button in the top-right corner.

A Customization Window with many parts will now show up. To customize your report, you can use a variety of filters, some of which are only available for certain reports. We will go through the following Sections in the Customization Window to build QuickBooks Custom Reports:

General settings

Here, you may choose the time frame for which the report's data should be displayed. Choose the Number format to standardize your data. There are two accounting methods available to you: Cash and Accrual.

Rows and Columns

You can select how the Data is shown in the columns and rows in this area. For instance, go to the Rows and Columns settings and select Months as your option in the Columns box for the Profit and Loss Reports for the months of January through March. These QuickBooks Custom Reports will show different columns for January, February, and March's Profit or Loss figures.

Additionally, you may add columns that show percentages and compare your profit and loss data to data from earlier periods, years, and the entire year. This can be useful if you own an online store and want to figure out what percentage of sales you spend on rent and utilities.

- Select the desired parameter by going to Rows/Columns > Change Columns.

Filter Section

This makes it easier for you to narrow down the report's target consumers, vendors, accounts, or goods. For instance, by following these steps, you may create QuickBooks Custom Reports for a Monthly Design Sales Report for all Accounts and Customers:

1. Select *Filter* from the menu.
2. Select *Design* for the products and services under *Lists*.

Header/Footer

You can set the Report Title, Company Name, date, and Time of Report Preparation, among other things, in this section once you have configured your QuickBooks Custom Report. Click *Run Report* after you're finished with this stage to create your QuickBooks Custom Reports.

Saving Individual Reports

Once you've finished applying all the criteria, don't forget to save the QuickBooks Custom Reports so you can use them as needed in the future. This is possible by:

1. Next to the *Customize* button in the top right corner, click the *Save Customization* button.
2. Give your report a name, then click *Save*.

Excel Exporting Reports

In some situations, you may discover that a report does not contain all the necessary columns. By transferring your QuickBooks Custom Reports into Microsoft Excel and manually inserting extra columns, you can incorporate data from additional reports. Select the *Export* icon and choose *Export to Excel* after running the report as indicated in the Green Box.

Limitations of Custom Reports and Dashboards

For custom invoices, cloud-based accounting, and accounting reports, QuickBooks is an exceptionally efficient tool. But there are several difficulties that you can run into when creating QuickBooks Custom Reports and Dashboards.

A QuickBooks Custom Report cannot be created from scratch. You can only partially customize the standard reports that come with QuickBooks. You may want to add columns from other reports in numerous circumstances. There is currently no such feature, so you must manually customize the reports after exporting them to Microsoft Excel. The dashboard's customizability is somewhat constrained.

Exporting Reports and Sending Via Email

Once the report is generated and customized to your requirements, the next step is to export it. QuickBooks Online facilitates the export of reports in various formats, including PDF and Excel. To initiate the export process, locate the export icon, often represented by a small arrow pointing upward, usually positioned at the top of the report page. Clicking on this icon will reveal a drop-down menu with export options.

Choose the desired export format based on your preferences. For instance, if you wish to share the report via email, selecting the PDF format is typically the best option, as it preserves the report's formatting and ensures the recipient views it exactly as intended.

Sending Reports via Email

After exporting the report, the next step is to send it via email to the relevant parties. Sending reports directly from QuickBooks Online is a convenient and time-saving feature. Begin the process by clicking on the email icon, often represented by an envelope, typically found alongside the export icon.

A new window will open, prompting you to enter the recipient's email address and any additional message or instructions you wish to include. You can also specify your email address as the sender, allowing recipients to respond directly to you with any queries or feedback.

Closing Periods

In the ever-evolving landscape of financial management, businesses face numerous challenges in maintaining accurate and reliable financial records. In this pursuit, accounting software like QuickBooks Online has emerged as a game-changer, streamlining financial reporting and analysis processes. One crucial aspect that significantly contributes to financial integrity and analysis efficiency is the concept of *closing periods*.

Step-by-step Guide to Closing a Financial Period in QuickBooks Online

QuickBooks Online offers a user-friendly and efficient process to close financial periods. Here's a step-by-step guide to help businesses navigate through the closing process:

Step 1: Backup Company File

Before initiating the closing process, it's prudent to back up the QuickBooks Online company file. This ensures that data remains safe in case of any unexpected technical issues during the closing process.

Step 2: Review Open Transactions

Review and resolve any open transactions in QuickBooks Online for the relevant period. These may include outstanding invoices, bills, or any other uncompleted financial activities. Ensure that all transactions are accurately recorded and categorized.

Step 3: Run Financial Statements

Generate the financial statements for the period that is about to be closed. Review the income statement, balance sheet, and cash flow statement for accuracy and completeness.

Step 4: Create Closing Journal Entries

QuickBooks Online allows users to create closing journal entries automatically. These entries help transfer the balances of temporary accounts, such as revenue and expenses, to the retained earnings account. This process resets the temporary accounts for the new period while preserving the historical data in the retained earnings account.

Step 5: Close the Period

Once all necessary adjustments and journal entries have been made, proceed to close the financial period in QuickBooks Online. This action will prevent any changes or additions to the closed period's financial data.

Step 6: Review and Confirm

Double-check all the closing entries and ensure that the closing process has been successfully executed. Verify that the closing balances are accurate and that the retained earnings account reflects the appropriate amount.

Step 7: Commence the New Period

With the previous period successfully closed, the books are now ready for the new period. Begin recording transactions for the new duration, ensuring that all entries are accurate and properly categorized.

Reviewing Transactions and Making Necessary Adjustments

During the closing process, it is crucial to conduct a thorough review of all financial transactions. This review involves verifying the accuracy of recorded transactions, ensuring that they are appropriately categorized, and identifying any discrepancies that require adjustment. Some key aspects to consider during this review include:

- **Revenue Recognition:** Confirm that revenue recognition follows the appropriate accounting principles and policies. For instance, revenue from long-term contracts may need to be recognized using the percentage-of-completion method.
- **Expense Allocation:** Check that expenses are allocated to the correct accounting periods. Certain expenses, such as prepaid insurance or deferred expenses, need to be adjusted to reflect the portion applicable to the current period accurately.
- **Inventory Valuation:** For businesses dealing with inventory, it's crucial to review inventory levels and reconcile them with physical counts. Any inconsistencies ought to be examined and appropriately rectified.

- **Depreciation and Amortization:** Review the depreciation and amortization schedules to ensure that these non-cash expenses are accurately recorded. Verify that the depreciation methods and useful lives used for assets align with accounting standards and company policies.
- **Accruals and Deferrals:** Evaluate accruals and deferrals to account for revenues or expenses that have been earned or incurred but not yet recorded. Adjustments should be made to recognize these items in the appropriate periods.

Reconciling Accounts and Ensuring Accuracy

Reconciliation is a crucial aspect of the closing process that ensures the accuracy and integrity of financial data. During this stage, various accounts, such as bank accounts, credit card accounts, and other balance sheet items, are reconciled to their respective statements or supporting documentation. Here's how to effectively reconcile accounts in QuickBooks Online:

- **Bank Reconciliation:** Perform bank reconciliation by comparing the transactions recorded in QuickBooks Online with bank statements. Resolve any discrepancies and ensure that the ending balances match.
- **Credit Card Reconciliation:** Similar to bank reconciliation, credit card accounts must be reconciled by comparing transactions in QuickBooks Online with credit card statements.
- **Balance Sheet Reconciliation:** Reconcile other balance sheet accounts, such as accounts receivable, accounts payable, and inventory, to ensure their accuracy and completeness.
- **Error Correction:** If any discrepancies are identified during the reconciliation process, promptly investigate and correct the errors. This may involve adjusting journal entries to rectify misclassifications or mis postings.

Chapter 10

Payroll and Employee Management

In the world of business, managing payroll and employee information is a critical aspect that can make or break an organization's success. Smooth and efficient payroll processes are essential to keep employees satisfied and maintain compliance with various tax regulations. QuickBooks Online (QBO), an acclaimed cloud-based accounting software developed by Intuit, offers a robust and user-friendly solution for payroll and employee management. In Chapter 10 of this comprehensive guide, we will delve into the intricacies of setting up and managing payroll in QuickBooks Online, including handling employee information, payroll taxes, and 1099 contractors.

Setting up Payroll in QBO

Step 1: Go to Payroll

You'll want to start by going to the *Payroll* tab after signing in to your QuickBooks account.

Hovering over the paycheck tab reveals three alternatives. You'll notice three choices when you hover your mouse over the *Payroll* tab: Employees, Contractors, and Workers' compensation. You can look into each of these possibilities, but we'll start with Employees. You'll notice a *Get Started* button if you recently purchased your QuickBooks Online membership. To go on to the next screen, simply click on it. The system will enquire about your needs for HR support and staff time tracking if you are merely signing up for QuickBooks Payroll.

Although these inquiries will aid in matching you with the appropriate plan, you also have the choice to manually choose one of its three payroll options. In addition to offering a 30-day free trial, QuickBooks will suggest the optimal payroll plan for you. Since the last time we updated this page, QuickBooks Payroll has introduced a *Contractor Payments* plan that is ideal for companies that recruit and pay exclusively contract employees. Up to 20 contractors may be hired for a monthly fee of $15 (plus $2 for each additional employee). Visit our QuickBooks Payroll review to learn more about the automated payroll and direct deposit functions of this software, as well as other capabilities that you and your staff might require.

Step 2: Provide General Payroll Information for Your Employees

The system will next ask you if you've already paid any employees for the current calendar year. You must select *Yes* if you're transferring to QuickBooks Payroll from a manual system or another payroll program. If *No* is selected, new companies that haven't yet processed their first paycheck should click *Next*. Keep in mind that the system will ask you to provide year-to-date (YTD) payroll information as well as any employee tax payments received later on in the setup process. In order to guarantee that your W-2 forms are valid at year-end, you must provide information on earlier paychecks that were sent to employees before the start of your QuickBooks Payroll subscription.

You can obtain YTD data for each employee from the most recent payroll you processed, and you can also ask your former payroll provider for specific pay reports. The system will ask you to specify the date that you intend to conduct your first payroll in QuickBooks, along with payments to employees in the current fiscal year. You will also need to provide the physical address of the workplace where the majority of your employees are located.

Step 3: Add Workers

Once you've entered your workplace, a new window will open up where you can enter the basic data and payroll information for your employees. Click the *Add an employee* button to begin entering the necessary information for each person on your payroll, including any individuals who have left your company but were compensated during the current fiscal year.

Step 4: Complete the Employee Data

You can enter your employees' email addresses as you enter basic employee data into QuickBooks. This enables the system to provide them with a link so they may use the provider's self-service web portal, QuickBooks Workforce, to examine their pay stubs and W-2s. Even better, the solution has the ability to ask workers to log their work hours using QuickBooks Time.

To utilize the time tracking tool QuickBooks Time, you must, however, be a member of one of QuickBooks Payroll's premium plans. The employee information fields that you must complete for the QuickBooks Online Payroll setup are listed below.

Pay schedule: In the *How often do you pay (employee)* area, select the *create pay schedule button* to specify a pay schedule for your staff members. Select the appropriate schedule from the dropdown menu, including weekly, bi-monthly and monthly, among others. Additionally, you will have the option of setting the newly established schedule as the default schedule for any future employees that are added to the system.

Pay for workers: The *How much do you pay (employee)* area should be filled out using the employee's salary. You must also enter the staff's default workdays and hourly rate for each day.

Contributions and deductions made by employees: Check the boxes next to the appropriate contribution and deduction items in the *Does the employee Have Any deductions?* section.

A worker who withholds information: The information from Form W-4s should be used in the *What are the employee's withholdings?* section. When you click *Enter W-4 form*, make a choice as to whether you need the tax form for the current year or one from a previous year. As of the date of this writing, the form was modified in December 2020, and QuickBooks keeps both the most recent and previous versions. This allows for direct printing of one from the system to be handed to staff, while also capturing the necessary data.

Payroll data as of the date: If you paid the employee this year, enter the YTD payroll information into the system using the data from the last payroll check you issued. Pay attention to the fact that QuickBooks will request totals paid for previous fiscal quarters as well as any sums paid during the current quarter before you start using QuickBooks Payroll.

Method of payment: You can choose between direct deposit and (manual) check in the *How do you want to pay (employee)* section's dropdown menu. If you choose direct deposit, enter the data from the authorization form for direct deposit and the employee's canceled check.

You must make sure the YTD totals are correct, which is crucial. To make sure that your reporting is accurate and trustworthy, this information will be essential. Additionally, it will affect annual maximums for federal and state taxes, such as 401(k) and retirement plan contribution caps. Check out our tutorial on how to process payroll for more information on contribution and deduction restrictions.

You'll see a list of employees on your payroll for the entire year once you've entered all the relevant data for each employee. Make sure all of the payment information is accurate by carefully reading it. Click the *Add an employee* option to add any new employees you may have or to add someone you may have forgotten.

If you see something on the list that needs to be changed, click the employee's name to make the necessary changes. Remember to configure your company's tax details after adding employees to the system. You can now execute your first pay run after finishing the payroll setup in QuickBooks. To process payroll in QuickBooks Online, adhere to these instructions:

Step 5: Select Run Payroll

Click the *Run payroll* button on your *Payroll* dashboard, which is in the top-right corner of the screen.

Step 6: Enter the Present Time

It should be noted that the system will automatically fill in the total hours for salaried employees based on the initial setup's default value for the employee's number of work hours. For hourly workers, you must manually enter their actual working hours in the *Regular Pay Hrs.* column or import their time information from your time tracking software.

If you use QuickBooks Time, which is integrated into both tiers of QuickBooks Payroll, to record and monitor employee attendance, your staff's work hours will automatically show in QuickBooks Payroll, ready for your evaluation and approval. Do not hesitate to update the system with any changes to the staff's work schedule. All hourly employees' hours can be entered from the payroll screen. For salaried workers, you will only see the total amount owing for that period of time; you won't see the number of hours worked.

Step 7: Examine and Submit the Payroll

The payroll data can be reviewed and edited one last time before being submitted. Check the payment method in addition to the number of hours worked and other compensation information to make sure that employees who should get direct deposits and paychecks do so. Review the tax amounts paid by the employer and the employee as well. Click the *Preview Payroll* button at the bottom right of the screen once you have finished examining your employee's time records and pay details. Provide direct deposit information in QuickBooks Payroll. You may enter an employee's direct deposit information while processing payroll with QuickBooks Payroll, and you can even switch between direct deposit and paycheck payments.

Click the *Submit Payroll* button located at the bottom right of the screen after you are certain that everything is accurate. Following this, you have the option to print payroll checks and/or direct deposit remittance advice to provide to your staff. A bill will be generated immediately for each payroll completed if you use QuickBooks Online as your accounting software, which makes it simple to reconcile your payroll account.

Managing Employee Information and Pay

Managing employee information and pay is a vital element in the successful operation of a business. It involves maintaining accurate records of employees' personal details, employment history, and compensation, as well as processing payroll efficiently. QuickBooks Online (QBO) offers a user-friendly and efficient solution for managing employee information and pay. In this section, we will outline the full procedure of managing employee information and pay in QuickBooks Online.

Step 1: Accessing Payroll Settings in QuickBooks Online

To begin managing employee information and pay in QuickBooks Online, log in to your QBO account and navigate to the *Employees* tab on the dashboard. From the dropdown menu, select *Payroll Settings*. This will lead you to the payroll management section, where you can set up and manage employee information and pay.

Step 2: Setting Up Employee Information

Once you are in the payroll settings section, you can start by adding employee information. Click on *Add Employee* to enter the necessary details. This includes the employee's full name, address, contact information, Social Security Number (SSN), and tax withholding allowances. It is essential to ensure that all information entered is accurate and up to date.

Step 3: Specifying Employment Details

After entering personal information, proceed to specify the employee's employment details. This includes the employee's start date, job title, employment status (full-time, part-time, or contractor), and work hours per week. If the employee is eligible for overtime, you can set up the overtime policy here as well.

Step 4: Setting Up Compensation and Payroll Schedule

The next step is to set up the employee's compensation details. Enter the wage rate, whether hourly or salary-based, and select the pay frequency (weekly, bi-weekly, semi-monthly, or monthly). QuickBooks Online allows you to be flexible with compensation options, accommodating various pay structures and frequencies.

Step 5: Managing Deductions and Contributions

In this step, you can manage deductions and contributions for the employee. Deductions may include health insurance premiums, retirement contributions, and other withholdings. Similarly, contributions may involve employer-matching retirement plans or other benefits. QuickBooks Online automatically calculates these deductions and contributions during payroll processing.

Step 6: Initiating Payroll Processing

With the employee information set up, you are now ready to process payroll. Go to the *Run Payroll* section within QuickBooks Online. Here, you will find a list of all active employees for whom you need to process payments. Verify that all details are accurate and up to date before proceeding.

Step 7: Reviewing and Confirming Payroll Details

Before finalizing payroll, review the pay details for each employee. QuickBooks Online provides a clear breakdown of wages, taxes, deductions, and net pay for each individual. Ensure that all numbers are correct and that any overtime hours or additional payments are accurately accounted for.

Step 8: Initiating Payroll Payment

Once you have confirmed the payroll details for all employees, you can initiate the payment process. QuickBooks Online offers multiple payment methods, including direct deposit and printing physical paychecks. Choose the appropriate payment method based on your employees' preferences and your business's requirements.

Step 9: Generating Paystubs and Reports

After completing the payroll payment process, QuickBooks Online generates paystubs for each employee. These paystubs outline the detailed breakdown of the employee's pay, including earnings, taxes, and deductions. Additionally, you can access various payroll reports to gain insights into labor costs, tax liabilities, and other payroll-related metrics.

Step 10: Keeping Employee Records Updated

Employee information is not static, and changes may occur over time, such as address updates, salary adjustments, or changes in tax withholding allowances. It is essential to keep employee records updated in QuickBooks Online to ensure accurate payroll processing and compliance with tax regulations.

Handling Payroll Taxes and Filings

Managing payroll taxes and filings is a crucial aspect of payroll and employee management for any business. QuickBooks Online offers a user-friendly and efficient solution to handle these tasks seamlessly. This procedure outlines the step-by-step process of handling payroll taxes and filings in QuickBooks Online, ensuring compliance with tax regulations and avoiding potential penalties.

Step 1: Verify Payroll Tax Setup

Before processing payroll and tax filings, it's essential to verify that the payroll tax setup in QuickBooks Online is accurate. To do this, log in to your QuickBooks Online account and navigate to the *Taxes* tab.

Step 2: Check Tax Identification Numbers

Ensure that your business's tax identification numbers, such as the Federal Employer Identification Number (FEIN) and state tax identification numbers, are correctly entered into the system. Any errors in these numbers could lead to inaccurate tax calculations and filings.

Step 3: Review Employee Information

Double-check that all employee information, including names, addresses, Social Security Numbers (SSNs), and tax withholding allowances, are up to date and accurate. Accurate employee data is crucial for calculating payroll taxes correctly.

Step 4: Set Up Payroll Tax Items

In QuickBooks Online, you need to set up payroll tax items corresponding to the different types of taxes your business needs to withhold and remit. Common payroll tax items include federal and state income taxes, Social Security, Medicare, and unemployment taxes.

Step 5: Assign Payroll Tax Items to Employees

Once the payroll tax items are set up, assign the appropriate tax items to each employee based on their tax withholding status. QuickBooks Online allows you to customize tax deductions for each employee, depending on their individual circumstances.

Step 6: Process Payroll

Process payroll for your employees in QuickBooks Online, ensuring that you accurately input the hours worked, wage rates, and any additional earnings or deductions. The system will automatically calculate the payroll taxes based on the assigned tax items and employee information.

Step 7: Review Payroll Summary

After processing payroll, review the payroll summary to ensure accuracy. Verify that the calculated payroll taxes match the amounts specified by the tax items and that there are no discrepancies.

Step 8: Submit Payroll Taxes and Filings

QuickBooks Online offers the option to electronically file federal and state payroll tax forms directly from the platform. To do this, navigate to the *Taxes* tab and select the appropriate tax form for the filing period. Follow the on-screen instructions to submit the form electronically to the respective tax authorities.

Step 9: Make Tax Payments

QuickBooks Online also allows businesses to make tax payments electronically. After submitting the tax forms, review the payment information and authorize the payment to be debited from your designated bank account.

Step 10: Generate Employee W-2 Forms

At the end of the tax year, QuickBooks Online facilitates the generation of employee W-2 forms. These forms summarize the employees' annual earnings and tax withholdings. Review the W-2 forms for accuracy and distribute them to your employees.

Step 11: Issue 1099 Forms to Contractors (if applicable)

For businesses working with 1099 contractors, QuickBooks Online simplifies the process of generating and filing Form 1099-NEC. Enter the contractor payments made throughout the year, and the platform will automatically generate the necessary 1099 forms.

Step 12: Reconcile Payroll Taxes

Regularly reconcile payroll tax liabilities in QuickBooks Online to ensure that the amounts withheld and paid match the reported figures on your tax forms. Reconciliation helps identify and resolve any discrepancies promptly.

QuickBooks Online (QBO) is a powerful accounting software that simplifies the process of managing 1099 contractors for businesses. 1099 contractors, also known as independent contractors or freelancers, play a crucial role in various industries. As a business owner, ensuring proper management of payments and tax reporting for 1099 contractors is essential to stay compliant with tax regulations. In this comprehensive guide, we will walk you through the step-by-step procedure of managing and setting up 1099 contractors in QuickBooks Online.

Setting up 1099 Contractors in QuickBooks Online

Step 1: Access the Contractor Center
1. Log in to your QuickBooks Online account using your login details.
2. Once logged in, navigate to the *Contractors* tab on the QBO dashboard.

Step 2: Add a New Contractor
1. In the Contractor Center, click on the *Add a contractor* button or a similar option, depending on the version of QBO you are using.

2. A form will appear where you can enter the contractor's details. Provide accurate information, including the contractor's full name, address, and Social Security Number (SSN) or Employer Identification Number (EIN).

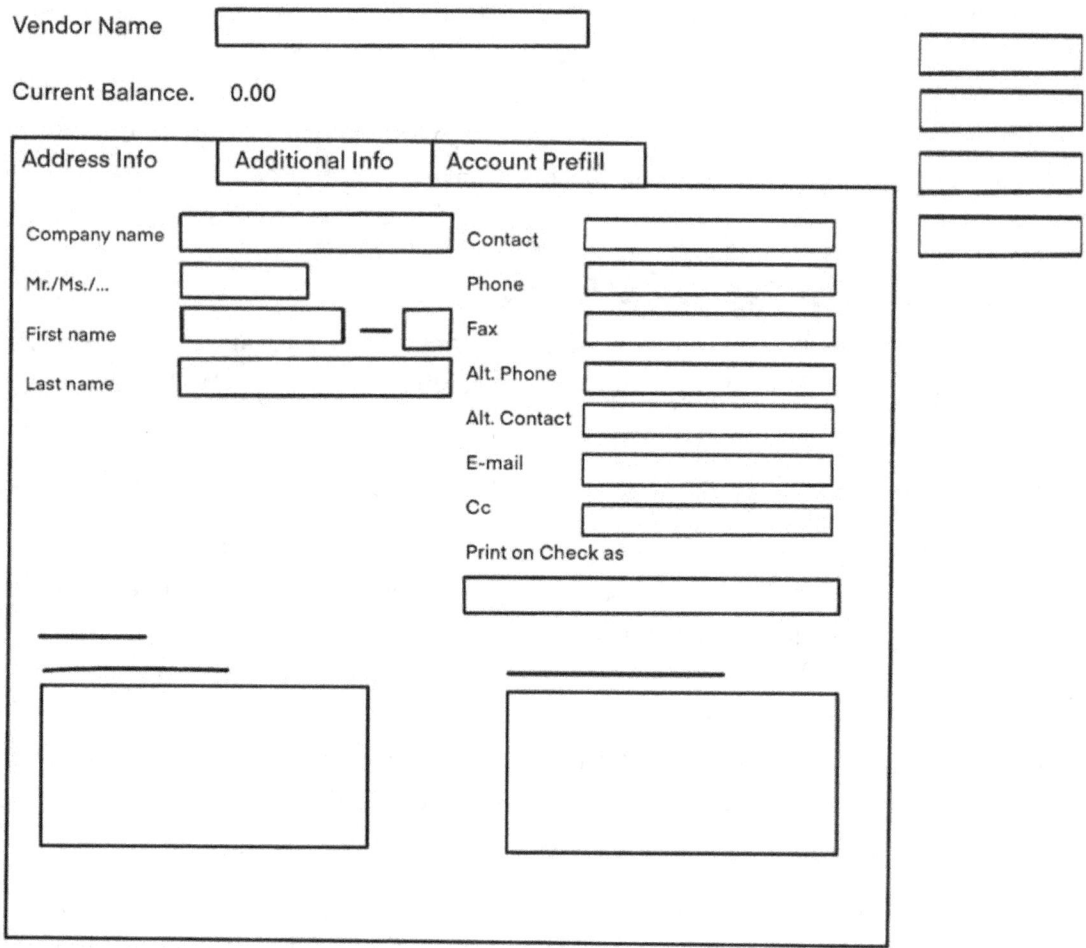

Step 3: Set up the Payment Method

1. After entering the contractor's information, proceed to set up the preferred payment method. Common payment methods include direct deposit or physical checks.
2. If the contractor opts for direct deposit, you will need to collect their bank account details, including routing and account numbers.

Step 4: Review and Save Contractor Information

1. Double-check all the information you have entered to ensure its accuracy.
2. Once you are satisfied with the details, click on the *Save* or *Save Contractor* button to add the 1099 contractor to QuickBooks Online.

Managing 1099 Contractors in QuickBooks Online

Step 1: Record Payments to Contractors

1. From the QBO dashboard, click on the *Expenses* tab and choose *Vendors* from the drop-down menu.
2. Select the *Pay Bills* option or similar, depending on your QBO version.
3. Choose the contractor you wish to make a payment to from the list of vendors.
4. Enter the payment amount and the date of payment.
5. If you are paying the contractor via direct deposit, select the appropriate bank account for the transaction.
6. Click on the *Save* or *Pay* button to record the payment.

Step 2: Track Payments to Contractors

1. To review past payments made to a specific contractor, access the *Expenses* tab and select *Vendors* from the drop-down menu.
2. Locate and click on the contractor's name to view their payment history.

How to Generate 1099-NEC Forms for Contractors

Step 1: Verify Contractor Payment Information

1. Before the end of the tax year, ensure that all payments made to 1099 contractors are accurately recorded in QuickBooks Online.

Step 2: Review and Confirm Contractor Information

1. Access the *Contractors* tab from the QBO dashboard and select the appropriate contractor's name.
2. Verify that the contractor's name, address, and tax identification number (SSN or EIN) are correct and up-to-date.

Step 3: Generate 1099-NEC Forms

1. QuickBooks Online provides an automated feature to generate 1099-NEC forms for contractors at the end of the tax year.
2. Access the *Taxes* tab from the QBO dashboard and select *Prepare 1099s* or similar, depending on your QBO version.
3. Follow the on-screen prompts to confirm contractor payment details and review the generated 1099-NEC forms for accuracy.
4. If everything is correct, select the option to file the forms electronically or print and mail them to the respective contractors.

Chapter 11

Taxes

Taxes are an integral part of any business, and understanding how to manage them efficiently is crucial for maintaining financial compliance and accuracy. In QuickBooks Online, a popular accounting software used by businesses worldwide, there are comprehensive tools and features available to streamline the process of setting up tax rates, creating invoices with sales tax, managing tax reports, and handling payroll taxes and filings. In this chapter, we will delve into these various aspects of tax management in QuickBooks Online, providing step-by-step guidance and practical insights to help businesses navigate the complexities of tax compliance.

Setting up Tax Rates

<Add New>

East Bayshore	Sales Tax Item	City Sales Tax
Out of State	Sales Tax Item	Out of state sales, exempt from sales tax
San Domingo	Sales Tax Item	CAsales tax, San Domingo County
San Tomas	Sales Tax Item	CAsales tax, San Tomas County
E. Bayshore County	Sales Tax Group	Sales Tax

(8.05%)	2,227,44
TOTAL	29,897.4r
PAYMENTS APPLIED	0.00
BALANCE DUE	29,897.44

Before delving into the details of handling taxes in QuickBooks Online, it is essential to set up accurate and relevant tax rates for your business. The process of setting up tax rates is straightforward and can be tailored to the specific requirements of your business and the locations in which you operate.

In QuickBooks Online, navigate to the *Taxes* tab and select *Sales Tax* from the drop-down menu. From there, you can add new tax rates by providing the tax name, rate, agency, and effective date. Additionally, you have the option to set up special tax rules based on specific criteria, such as customer location or product type. Ensuring that tax rates are set up accurately is crucial to avoid any discrepancies in tax calculations in the future.

Creating an Invoice with Sales Tax

Once tax rates are set up, the next step is to create invoices that include sales tax. QuickBooks Online allows you to automate the calculation of sales tax on invoices, making the process more efficient and accurate.

To create an invoice with sales tax, simply add the products or services sold to the invoice, and QuickBooks Online will automatically calculate the applicable sales tax based on the customer's location and the tax rates set up in the system. This removes the necessity for hand-done calculations and lowers the chances of mistakes, ensuring that your invoices are accurate and comply with tax regulations.

Collecting Sales Tax

Collecting sales tax from customers is a crucial responsibility for businesses. It is important to clearly communicate to customers the inclusion of sales tax in their invoices and ensure that the collected tax is appropriately recorded and accounted for.

When you create invoices in QuickBooks Online with the automated sales tax calculation, the sales tax amount is displayed separately on the invoice. This transparency helps customers understand the taxes they are paying, fostering trust and compliance. Once you receive payments from customers, QuickBooks Online will automatically track and record the sales tax amounts, simplifying the process of sales tax collection and ensuring accurate financial records.

Creating Invoice Templates

QuickBooks Online offers flexibility in customizing invoice templates to suit your business needs. Apart from displaying sales tax information, you can create templates with subtotals for labor and materials, allowing you to present a comprehensive breakdown of the invoice amount.

Moreover, if your business charges service fees based on a percentage of the invoice total, QuickBooks Online enables you to add this service fee percentage to each invoice automatically. This feature streamlines the invoicing process, ensures consistency in applying service fees, and eliminates the need for manual adjustments.

Paying Sales Tax

As a business, it is essential to keep track of the sales tax you collect from customers and set aside these funds for tax payments to the appropriate tax agencies. QuickBooks Online simplifies this process by providing a clear overview of the sales tax amounts collected and the tax liabilities accrued.

To pay sales tax in QuickBooks Online, navigate to the *Taxes* tab and select *Sales Tax*. From there, you can review the sales tax amounts collected and the corresponding tax payments due. QuickBooks Online also allows you to make tax payments directly through the platform, streamlining the process and reducing the risk of missed deadlines or errors in tax payments.

Pay sales taxes				X
Pay from account	**Check Date**	**Show sales tax due through**		**Starting Check No.**
————	————	————		——

P...	Item	Vendor	Amt. due	Amt. paid
✓	———————	———————	——	——
✓	——————	——————	——	——
✓	————	——————	——	——
		——————	——————	——————
		——————	——————	——————

Creating Tax Reports

Accurate and comprehensive tax reporting is crucial for businesses to assess their tax liabilities, analyze financial performance, and ensure compliance with tax regulations. QuickBooks Online offers a range of tax reports that provide insights into different aspects of tax management.

Some of the key tax reports available in QuickBooks Online include Sales Tax Liability Report, Taxable Sales Report, and Tax Payments Report. These reports offer detailed breakdowns of tax amounts collected, taxable sales, and tax payments made over specific periods, enabling businesses to analyze their tax data effectively.

Handling Payroll Taxes and Filings

Managing payroll taxes and filings is a significant responsibility for businesses with employees. QuickBooks Online offers features and tools to simplify the process of handling payroll taxes, ensuring accuracy and compliance.

In QuickBooks Online Payroll, you can set up payroll tax preferences based on your business's location and specific tax requirements. The platform will automatically calculate payroll taxes, including federal and state income taxes, Social Security, Medicare, and unemployment taxes, based on employee wages and tax rates. Moreover, QuickBooks Online facilitates the electronic filing of payroll taxes, saving time and reducing the risk of errors associated with manual filings.

Chapter 12

Integration and Additional Features

QuickBooks Online (QBO), the cloud-based accounting software developed by Intuit, has long been a favored choice for small and medium-sized enterprises (SMEs) due to its user-friendly interface and comprehensive financial management features. However, QBO's potential doesn't end there. In Chapter 12, we will delve into the world of integration and additional features that can take your QBO experience to new heights.

Exploring Third-Party Integrations

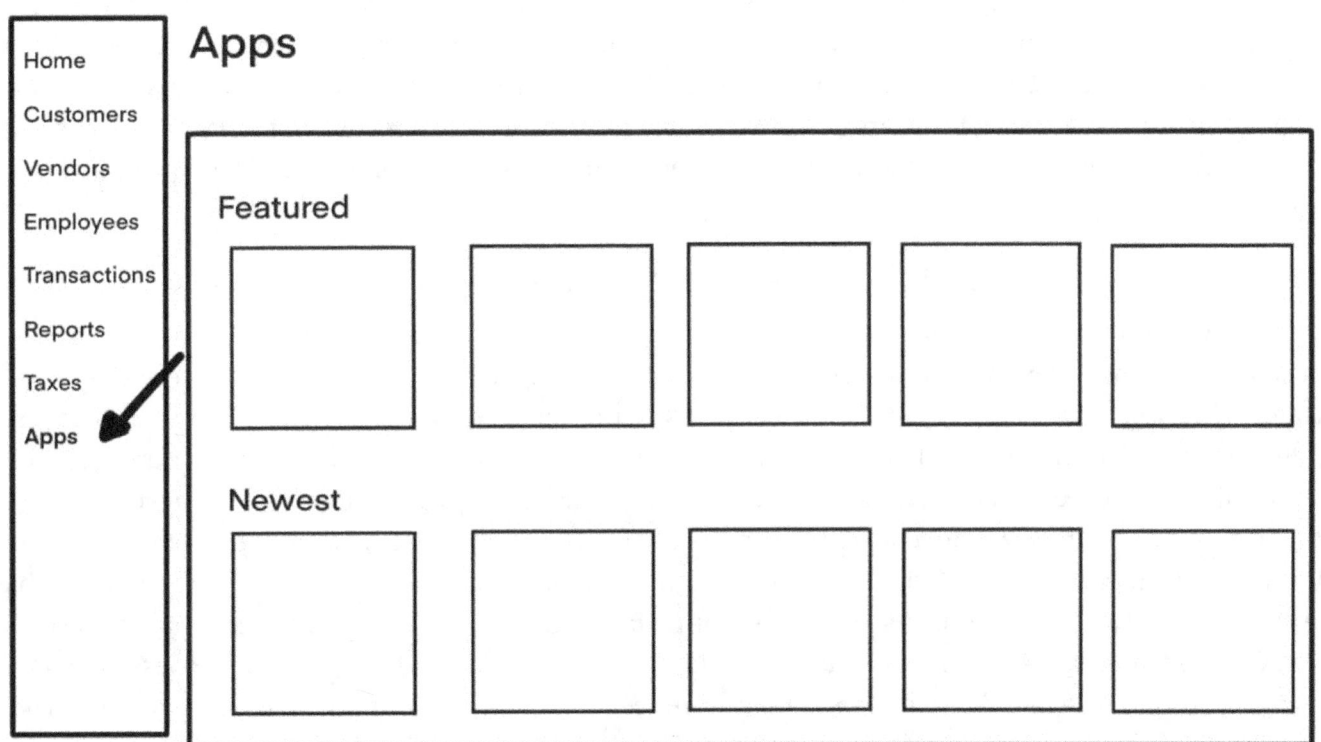

What Are QuickBooks Online Best Integration Tools?

QuickBooks accountants, your life is about to get much simpler as a result of our compilation of the top QuickBooks Integration tools. It might take a significant amount of time and money to create the ideal financial IT stack for your business. For CFOs who use QuickBooks Online as their accounting software, we have put together our suggestions for the best fintech stack.

Find out how users integrate QuickBooks Online with other platforms like Tallie, Bill.com, and Procurify.

Benefits of QuickBooks Integration

By removing hours of manual data entry, connecting third-party software platforms with QuickBooks helps businesses save time. For a good reason, QuickBooks interacts with more than 650 widely used business software programs. In other words, by eliminating manual data entry activities from your accounting procedures, you'll save a ton of time. With integrations, all data is often immediately synced into QuickBooks from other platforms, making QuickBooks your one source of truth for all data. Consequently, consumers of QuickBooks integrations:

- Spend less time entering data
- Less tense month-end closings
- Improving the accrual procedure
- Improve operational and financial oversight
- Streamline digital approval processes.
- Highlighted QuickBooks Tools for Online Integration

Procurify

Procurify is first revolutionizing how businesses spend. Software that is easy to use, quick to install, and intuitive is available through Procurify. Procurify streamlines the process from onboarding to product training and support. For USA-made goods, Procurify provides direct connectivity with all QuickBooks Online tiers. This interface transfers bill data from Procurify to QuickBooks Online to assist teams in confidently verifying invoices, saving hours on data entry, and streamlining month-end by synchronizing all attachments.

The Best QuickBooks Online Integration Tools

Second, Bill.com is a provider of cloud-based software for small and medium enterprises that streamlines back-office financial operations. To assist businesses in managing their cash inflows and outflows, the company's AI-enabled platform connects them with their clients and suppliers. Bill.com links to banks and integrates with QuickBooks Online, Pro, Premier, and Enterprise to streamline payments and expedite reconciliation. Last but not least, Tallie is humanizing work by giving employees, approvers, financial experts, and CFOs the power to minimize labor-intensive, manual activities. They may then concentrate on what really matters. Some of the most potent and reliable cost management and accounts payable automation systems are combined in Emburse. For instance, Tallie, Chrome River, Abacus, Captio, Nexonia, and Certify. More than 4.5 million consumers and finance leaders in more than 120 countries rely on the company's solutions. In order to minimize manual procedures, lower risk, assure compliance, and provide deep spend insights to enable wiser, more informed decisions, over 14,000 organizations rely on Emburse's solutions.

Leveraging QBO Apps and Add-Ons

Numerous add-ons and programs are available in QuickBooks® Online that seamlessly integrate to automate processes such as data entry, bookkeeping, and workflows. These straightforward QuickBooks allow small and medium-sized businesses to function more effectively.

QuickBooks Online Advanced users can benefit from an ever – expanding library of Premium Applications, which offer access to all your essential data in one easy to access location. Thanks to these adaptable solutions, business owners can avoid the time-consuming task of manually inputting numbers and information. Instead, these integrations increase efficiency and turn QuickBooks into the one place you need to go for all of your financial and business information.

Locating the perfect application or add-on for your business is challenging due to the vast selection available in the QuickBooks App Store. Therefore, we have put together a selection of the top QuickBooks applications and add-ons suited to your specific needs and business. Check out the QuickBooks Online Advanced collection of Premium Apps for a streamlined experience with bookkeeping, accounting, payroll, and other financial processes.

Advanced QuickBooks Online Premium Apps

Bill.com

Bill.com is one of the most popular tools available for QuickBooks syncing. With Bill.com, you can create personalized processes and routing rules for quicker and simpler approvals from any device, giving you greater control over your finances. To manage your accounts payable and receivable, you can use the Bill.com interface to sync all of your bank account data with QuickBooks. You can enable the Premium App-only feature of deep linkage between bills in both programs when you link Bill.com to your QuickBooks Online Advanced account.

Your invoices, clients, accounts, book balance, and vendors are synced while using Bill.com with QuickBooks. You may set reminders, automate approvals, and more with this functionality. You can even schedule payments. The Bill.com app will allow you to quickly access any bills that require your attention.

HubSpot

It's essential to integrate HubSpot with your customer relationship management (CRM) program. You can view all of your prospects and customers' information in one location with HubSpot and QuickBooks. One of the greatest QBO connectors is HubSpot, which allows companies to integrate their accounting and CRM systems to streamline the sales process and enhance collaboration between sales and finance teams. Customers can import draught invoices into QuickBooks Online Advanced and set up their own automated flow to transport draught invoices from HubSpot to Advance for inspection and approval using the HubSpot integration available as a Premium App.

Salesforce

Salesforce is a popular QuickBooks app as well. Salesforce enables you to link your CRM and accounting systems, so you can see how your company is doing and where it needs to improve. Only advanced users of QuickBooks Online have access to the company's premium app, the Salesforce Connector. It efficiently facilitates collaboration between your sales and finance teams, ensuring consistent data maintenance throughout accounts, invoices, and transactions. These two teams can also exchange information about customers, sales orders, expenses, and billing. You have total visibility into your company's operations and cash flow when these two platforms are combined. The connector gives you precise data in real-time to fuel business expansion.

DocuSign E-Sign

DocuSign E-Sign app Our collection of Premium Apps now includes DocuSign as the first e-Signature connection. Teams may locate signatures from customers, staff members, and other professionals with the DocuSign eSignature Connector for QuickBooks Online Advanced. Utilizing QuickBooks Online Advanced along with DocuSign eSignature allows for the straightforward signing, sending, and administration of digital documents. DocuSign e-signing for QuickBooks Online Advanced enables you to send estimates for electronic signing right from QuickBooks, making business easier for both you and your clients. Users of QuickBooks Online Advanced are the only ones who can access this integration.

LeanLaw

An industry-specific integration called LeanLaw increases productivity for law firms and other legal organizations. Because it offers the data and reporting you need as a law firm at your fingertips, we've ranked this as one of the top QuickBooks applications. A variety of activities, including billable hours, client reports, and trust accounting, among others, may be tracked thanks to the QuickBooks Online Advanced interface.

PayRoll for QuickBooks

Intuit® is the owner of QuickBooks Payroll, which integrates seamlessly with QuickBooks Online. You can pay and manage your workforce in one location with QuickBooks Payroll. Your go-to app for handling payday is QuickBooks Payroll, which integrates payroll, human resources, taxes, health benefits, workers' compensation, and more.

Additionally, auto-payroll, same-day direct deposit, and sophisticated mobile time tracking by QuickBooks Time are included with QuickBooks Payroll to make keeping track of hours and paying employees simple. Come tax season, QuickBooks Payroll can also be useful for small business owners. The most recent rates for sales tax, income tax, payroll tax, and other taxes are used in this software to process your payroll. Additionally, it automatically submits forms and calculates payments.

Various Other Well-Known Applications

Additional add-ons that can sync with your QuickBooks program are available in the QuickBooks App Store in addition to Premium Apps. Popular applications worth mentioning include:

Fathom

Fathom analyses your company's health by looking at cash flow, profitability, and other performance metrics. It is a must-have QuickBooks connection for any small or medium-sized firm. You will receive graphics of business intelligence data and trends as you use the Fathom app, including the financial and non-financial aspects of your firm. Once you have the knowledge, you can plan ahead and make decisions to address any problems head-on. Even better, users of QuickBooks Online Advanced receive a free Fathom subscription as part of their monthly Advanced subscription.

Buys from Amazon Business

A new app integration called Amazon Business Purchases is ideal for businesses looking for a quick way to import Amazon Business Purchase transactions into QuickBooks. By automatically obtaining the purchases each day, the Amazon Business app avoids human data entry and saves time. After that, you can evaluate and balance these purchases in QuickBooks. Additionally, the app offers information about each transaction, including item costs, product pricing, and charge splits. When you have these facts, you can classify them, organize them into groups, and compare them to your bank transactions to improve your spending management.

Expensify

One of the top QuickBooks add-ons, Expensify, is highly recommended. Employees may easily claim items as expenses with Expensify. Employees may quickly get their charges approved by taking a picture of the receipt, whether it's for gas or a client lunch charged on a business credit card.

For quick and simple approval, Expensify's SmartScan technology extracts data from receipts, such as the merchant's name, dates, and spending amounts, and integrates it into QuickBooks. The practice of saving paper receipts for weeks at a time is no longer practiced. To help you with your cash flow, Expensify can handle your administrative tasks, keep track of your spending, and build you a receipt bank.

Magento

With Magento, you can monitor your inventory and sync your sales in a matter of minutes, saving you hours of tedious manual data entry. When an order is created in Magento, you may use one of the many helpful features it offers to create an invoice in QuickBooks Online. When a product is made in Magento, you may also make a new item in QuickBooks Online. In order to make sure that stock levels are up to date, Magento also enables you to create various sales channels that connect to QuickBooks Online and match products based on their names or SKUs. Magento is the best choice for efficient inventory management.

Advanced Features and Tips

Uncovering Hidden Gems in QBO

QuickBooks Online, with its user-friendly interface and robust financial management features, is already a powerful tool. However, beneath the surface, QBO harbors a treasure trove of lesser-known but highly useful features. By unearthing these hidden gems, users can elevate their accounting processes to a whole new level.

- **Bank Feeds and Rules:** QBO's Bank Feeds feature allows users to connect their bank accounts and credit cards directly to the software. It automatically imports transactions, saving considerable time on manual data entry. To further streamline this process, users can set up Bank Rules. These rules automatically categorize transactions based on predefined criteria, ensuring consistent and accurate bookkeeping.

- **Batch Transactions:** When dealing with repetitive tasks, like invoicing a group of customers for the same product or service, the Batch Transactions feature becomes invaluable. It allows users to create multiple transactions simultaneously, eliminating the need to input each one individually.
- **Recurring Transactions:** For expenses or income that occur regularly and predictably, QBO's Recurring Transactions feature comes to the rescue. Users can set up templates for recurring invoices, bills, or journal entries, saving time and ensuring no important transactions are overlooked.
- **Custom Fields:** Businesses often have unique data they want to track that may not fit within QBO's default fields. Custom Fields enable users to add additional information to customers, vendors, and transactions, providing a more comprehensive view of their financial data.
- **Audit Log:** Maintaining data security and accountability is critical for any business. The Audit Log feature in QBO keeps track of all user activities and changes made within the system, helping to trace any modifications and monitor user actions.

Pro Tips for Optimal QBO Usage

To make the most of QuickBooks Online capabilities, here are some expert tips that can enhance efficiency and accuracy in financial management:

- **Regular Data Backups:** It's essential to perform regular backups of QBO data to safeguard against potential data loss due to technical issues or human errors. Utilizing Intuit's data backup services or third-party solutions can provide peace of mind and ensure business continuity.
- **Utilize Class and Location Tracking:** For businesses with multiple departments, projects, or locations, Class and Location Tracking can be invaluable. By categorizing transactions using these features, businesses can gain deeper insights into their financial performance across different segments.
- **Integration with Inventory Management:** If a business handles inventory, integrating QBO with an inventory management system can optimize stock control and order management. This integration helps avoid stockouts, overstocking, and discrepancies in inventory records.
- **Set User Permissions:** QBO allows administrators to customize user permissions, limiting access to sensitive financial data. By setting appropriate user roles and permissions, businesses can ensure that employees have access only to the information they need to perform their tasks.
- **Utilize Reports and Dashboards:** QBO offers a wide range of pre-built reports and customizable dashboards. Regularly reviewing these reports can provide valuable insights into financial performance, cash flow, and key performance indicators (KPIs).
- **Stay Updated on QBO Enhancements:** Intuit frequently releases updates and new features to improve QBO. Staying informed about these enhancements and attending webinars or training sessions can help users leverage the latest tools and functionalities.

Chapter 13

Mastering Journal Entries in QBO for Beginners

QuickBooks Online (QBO), a widely used cloud-based accounting software, offers a user-friendly platform for businesses to manage their finances efficiently. However, understanding and mastering journal entries in QBO can be a daunting task for beginners. This chapter aims to demystify the process, providing a step-by-step guide on creating journal entries, comprehending debits and credits, selecting the appropriate accounts for transactions, and utilizing descriptions and memos effectively.

What are Journal Entries?

Journal entries are the fundamental building blocks of the double-entry accounting system. They provide a chronological record of financial transactions, such as sales, purchases, expenses, and other monetary movements within a business. Each entry consists of two components: a debit and a credit, where the total amount of debits must always equal the total amount of credits, ensuring the accounting equation (Assets = Liabilities + Equity) remains balanced.

The purpose of journal entries extends beyond mere data entry; they serve as a comprehensive audit trail, allowing businesses to trace the origin of every financial transaction. Additionally, journal entries facilitate the preparation of financial statements, such as the balance sheet, income statement, and cash flow statement, providing crucial insights into a company's financial health.

Step-by-Step Guide to Creating a Journal Entry

QuickBooks Online (QBO) is a powerful cloud-based accounting software that simplifies financial management for businesses of all sizes. One of its essential features is the ability to create journal entries, which form the backbone of the double-entry accounting system. Journal entries are crucial for maintaining accurate financial records and preparing financial statements. In this step-by-step guide, we will walk you through the process of creating a journal entry in QBO, ensuring that you can confidently handle this critical aspect of accounting.

Step 1: Access the Journal Entry Form

To get started, log in to your QuickBooks Online account and ensure that you have the necessary access rights to create journal entries. Once logged in, navigate to the *Create* (+) menu, usually located in the upper-right corner of the screen. Under the *Other* section, you will find the option to *Journal Entry*. Click on it to access the journal entry form.

Step 2: Date the Entry

Once you are in the journal entry form, the first field you will encounter is the date field. It is essential to enter the correct date for the transaction being recorded. The date should reflect the actual date of the financial event, ensuring that your journal entries are organized chronologically.

Step 3: Choose Accounts and Enter Amounts

The heart of the journal entry lies in the accounts and their corresponding amounts. Begin by selecting the accounts that are involved in the transaction. These accounts can include assets, liabilities, equity, revenues, and expenses. For each account, determine whether it will be affected positively (debited) or negatively (credited) by the transaction.

For example, imagine your business made a cash sale of $500. In this case, you would select the *Cash* account and enter a debit of $500 to increase the cash account. Additionally, you would select the appropriate revenue account (e.g., *Sales* or *Service Income*) and enter a credit of $500 to record the increase in revenue.

It is essential to remember that the total of all debit amounts must equal the total of all credit amounts in the journal entry. This principle ensures that the accounting equation remains balanced.

Step 4: Add Descriptions and Memos

To provide clarity and context to your journal entry, it is essential to include detailed descriptions for each line item. Descriptions should be concise yet informative, explaining the nature of the transaction and any additional relevant information.

For instance, if the journal entry records a purchase of office supplies, the description could be *Office Supplies Purchase for Q2 - 2023*. This description not only explains the purpose of the entry but also makes it easier to identify the transaction when reviewing records in the future.

In addition to descriptions, QuickBooks Online allows you to add memos to each line item. Memos serve as internal notes that are not included in the financial statements but are helpful for internal record-keeping and communication within your organization. Memos can include further details, such as the names of involved parties or specific project names related to the transaction.

Step 5: Save the Journal Entry

Before finalizing the journal entry, it is crucial to review all the information carefully. Verify that the accounts, amounts, dates, descriptions, and memos are accurate and free of errors. This step ensures that your financial records are reliable and that you can easily trace the origin of each transaction.

Once you are satisfied with the journal entry, click the *Save* or *Save and Close* button, depending on your preferences. QuickBooks Online will then save the entry, and it will become part of your financial records.

Understanding Debits and Credits in Journal Entries

In the world of accounting, the concept of debits and credits is fundamental to the double-entry bookkeeping system. While this concept might appear daunting at first, grasping the essence of debits and credits is essential for any aspiring accountant or business owner. In this comprehensive explanation, we will demystify the notion of debits and credits in journal entries, providing clarity and understanding without the burden of jargon or confusion.

The Foundation of Double-Entry Accounting

The double-entry accounting system forms the bedrock of modern financial recording. It operates on a straightforward principle: every financial transaction has a dual impact on a company's accounts. In other words, for every debit made to one account, there must be an equivalent credit to another account. This principle ensures that the accounting equation, Assets = Liabilities + Equity, remains in balance, and no financial activity goes unaccounted for.

Debits and Credits: A Conceptual Framework

To comprehend debits and credits better, it is crucial to discard any preconceived notions of *increases* and *decreases*. In the context of journal entries, debits, and credits are not straightforward synonyms for *gain* and *loss*. Instead, they represent the direction in which the value of an account is affected by a transaction.

Debits

Debits are recorded on the left side of a journal entry and typically represent the following:

- **An increase in asset accounts:** Assets include cash, accounts receivable, inventory, equipment, and other tangible or intangible resources a company owns. For instance, when a business receives $1,000 in cash, it records a debit to the cash account to reflect the increase in available funds.
- **A decrease in liability accounts:** Liabilities encompass accounts payable, loans, and any obligations a company owes to external parties. When a company pays off a $500 loan, it records a debit to the loan liability account to signify a reduction in debt.
- **A decrease in equity accounts:** Equity accounts represent the owners' stake in the business, including common stock and retained earnings. If a company repurchases $300 worth of its own shares, it records a debit to the common stock account to indicate the reduction in shareholder equity.

Credits

Credits are documented on the right side of a journal entry and generally signify the following:

- **An increase in liability accounts:** When a business borrows $10,000 from a bank, it records a credit to the loan liability account to denote the rise in owed funds.
- **An increase in equity accounts:** If a company earns $5,000 in net profit, it records a credit to the retained earnings account to reflect the increase in overall owner's equity.
- **A decrease in asset accounts:** If a company sells goods worth $2,000, it records a credit to the inventory account to indicate the reduction in inventory value.

Recording Transactions Using Debits and Credits

To illustrate the application of debits and credits, let's consider a common business transaction: a company makes a $1,500 purchase of office supplies using cash. The journal entry for this transaction would be as follows:

Debit: Office Supplies (Asset Account) - $1,500 Credit: Cash (Asset Account) - $1,500

The debt to the *Office Supplies* account reflects the increase in the asset value, as the company now owns $1,500 worth of office supplies. Simultaneously, the credit to the *Cash* account demonstrates the decrease in available cash by the same amount.

Ensuring Balance: The Golden Rule of Accounting:

The key principle to remember when working with debits and credits is that the total dollar amount of debits must always equal the total dollar amount of credits in a journal entry. This adherence to balance is known as the *golden rule* of accounting.

Ensuring balance in each journal entry guarantees that the company's financial statements, such as the balance sheet and income statement, will present accurate information. It also helps auditors and stakeholders validate the financial records, thus fostering trust and transparency in the organization's financial health.

The Appropriate Accounts for Journal Entry Transactions

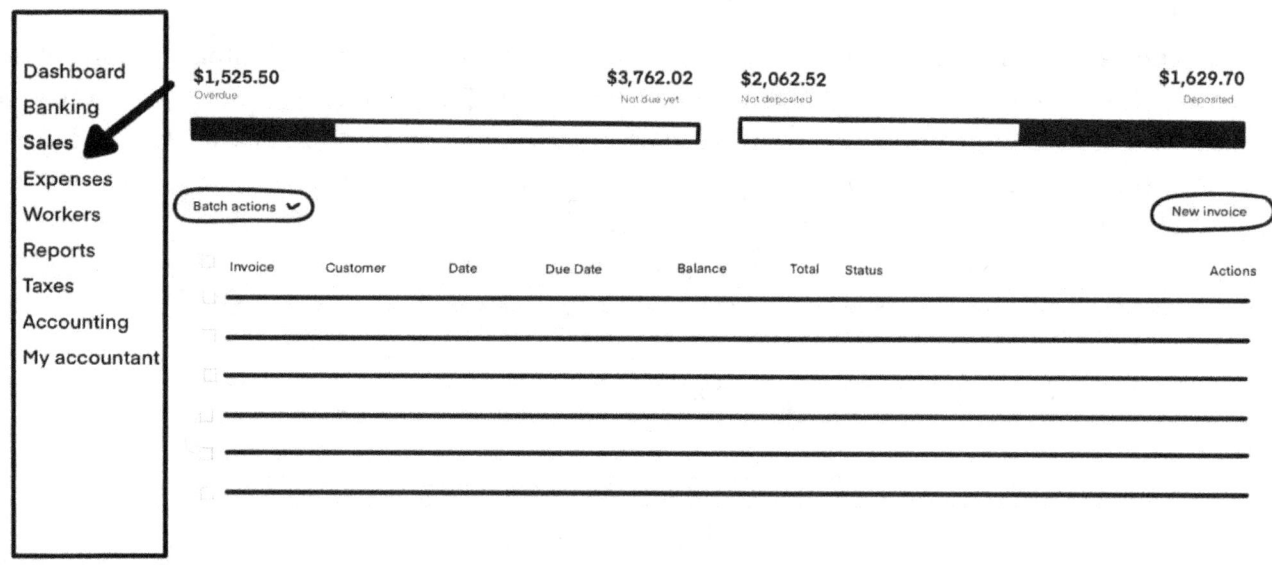

Selecting the right accounts for journal entries requires a clear understanding of the transaction's nature and its impact on the financial statements. Here are some common scenarios and the appropriate accounts to use:

- **Recording Sales:** Suppose your business makes a sale for $1,000. You would debit the cash or accounts receivable account (depending on whether the customer pays immediately or later) and credit the revenue account associated with the sale.
- **Handling Expenses:** If your company pays $500 for office supplies, you will debit the office supplies account and credit the cash account.
- **Loan Transactions:** When obtaining a loan of $10,000, you would debit the cash account (as the money is received) and credit the loan liability account.

- **Owner's Investment:** If the business owner invests $5,000 of personal funds into the company, you would debit the cash account and credit the owner's equity account.

Adding Descriptions and Memos in Journal Entries

While debits and credits are the foundation of journal entries, a crucial aspect of recording financial transactions is providing meaningful context through descriptions and memos. Descriptions serve as a concise explanation of the transaction, while memos offer additional details that aid in internal record-keeping and communication within the organization. In this comprehensive exploration, we will delve into the significance of descriptions and memos in journal entries, emphasizing their role in creating comprehensive and transparent financial records.

The Importance of Descriptions

In the world of accounting, clear and informative descriptions are invaluable. They provide essential context for each line item in a journal entry, enabling anyone reviewing the financial records to understand the nature and purpose of the transaction without ambiguity. A well-written description ensures that even complex transactions can be easily interpreted, aiding auditors, stakeholders, and financial analysts in their analysis.

For example, consider a journal entry recording a payment made to a vendor for office equipment. A generic description like *Vendor Payment* might not provide sufficient detail. In contrast, a descriptive entry such as *Payment to XYZ Office Supplies for New Office Chairs* gives a precise account of the transaction, making it easier to track and reference in the future.

Crafting Effective Descriptions

When writing descriptions for journal entries, accountants and bookkeepers should follow some best practices to ensure clarity and accuracy:

- **Be Specific:** Avoid vague terms and instead use precise language to convey the purpose of the transaction. Include relevant names, dates, and specific items involved.
- **Use Clear Language:** Keep the description succinct and straightforward, using simple language that is easily understandable to a diverse audience.
- **Include Relevant Information:** Incorporate any additional information that could be beneficial for analysis or future reference, such as project codes or customer names.

The Role of Memos

While descriptions provide the essential context for a transaction, memos serve as internal notes that are not part of the formal financial statements but are crucial for internal record-keeping and communication within the organization. Memos can include further details, explanations, or reminders related to the transaction.

For instance, suppose a company purchases equipment for a specific project. In this case, a memo associated with the journal entry could include project-specific information, such as the project's objective, milestones, or department responsible. This information aids project managers and stakeholders in tracking expenses and understanding the financial impact of each project.

Enhancing Transparency and Communication

Both descriptions and memos play a vital role in fostering transparency and communication within the organization. Transparent financial records enable stakeholders to gain insights into the company's financial activities, understand the decision-making process, and assess the organization's financial health.

Additionally, descriptions and memos facilitate seamless communication between different departments, enhancing collaboration and streamlining financial reporting. When financial records are clear and easily interpretable, it becomes simpler for teams to work together and make data-driven decisions.

Utilizing Accounting Software for Descriptions and Memos

Modern accounting software, such as QuickBooks Online, provides user-friendly interfaces for entering descriptions and memos in journal entries. Accountants and bookkeepers can easily input relevant information while creating journal entries, ensuring that the documentation is comprehensive and accurate.

Chapter 14

Troubleshooting and Time-Saving Tips

QuickBooks Online (QBO) has emerged as a leading cloud-based accounting solution. Its user-friendly interface and wide range of features make it a popular choice for entrepreneurs, small businesses, and accountants alike. However, like any software, QBO is not without its challenges. In this chapter, we will explore common issues that users may encounter while using QBO and provide step-by-step troubleshooting techniques to overcome them. Furthermore, we will delve into valuable tips and strategies to enhance efficiency and productivity when working with QBO, as well as time-saving shortcuts that will streamline the accounting process.

Common Issues and How to Troubleshoot Them

Connectivity Issues

In the digital age, a stable internet connection is the backbone of seamless accounting software usage. Unfortunately, connectivity issues can arise and hinder the smooth functioning of QuickBooks Online (QBO). Nothing can be more frustrating than being unable to access financial data or carry out essential tasks due to a faulty internet connection. When faced with connectivity problems, users can follow these practical troubleshooting steps to get QBO up and running again:

Check Internet Connection

The first step is to ensure that the internet connection is stable and working correctly. This can be done by accessing other websites or performing a speed test to verify the connection's reliability. If there are issues with other websites as well, the problem may lie with the internet service provider.

Clear Browser Cache

Over time, web browsers store temporary data such as cache and cookies. The accumulated cache can lead to unexpected errors and conflicts in QBO. To resolve this, users should clear the browser's cache and cookies. The process varies depending on the browser being used, but it can usually be found in the browser's settings or preferences section.

Try a Different Browser

Different web browsers handle websites and applications differently. If QBO is not functioning correctly in one browser, it is worth trying to access it using a different browser. Some common browsers include Google Chrome, Mozilla Firefox, Microsoft Edge, and Safari. Changing to a different browser can assist in establishing whether the issue is confined to a single browser or is a broader concern.

Disable Add-ons and Extensions

Browser extensions and add-ons can enhance the browsing experience, but they can also interfere with the functionality of web applications like QBO. Users should temporarily disable all extensions and add-ons and then attempt to use QBO again. If the issue is resolved, one of the disabled extensions may be causing the problem. Users can then re-enable each extension one by one to identify the culprit.

Check QBO Server Status

Intuit, the company behind QuickBooks Online, maintains the servers that host the application. Occasionally, there may be server issues or outages that affect QBO's performance. To check for any ongoing server problems, users can visit Intuit's website or participate in community forums dedicated to QBO. If the servers are down, users will have to wait until the issue is resolved by Intuit's technical team.

Syncing Problems

As businesses expand and rely on an ecosystem of applications to manage their finances, data synchronization becomes crucial. QBO allows users to integrate with various third-party apps, which can lead to data syncing problems. Here are steps to troubleshoot and address syncing issues effectively:

Verify Internet Connection

Like connectivity issues, ensuring a stable internet connection is essential for successful data synchronization. Confirm that all devices involved in the data exchange are connected to a reliable network.

Check App Integrations

Many businesses use third-party apps to enhance QBO's functionality. When syncing issues occur, it is vital to verify that these apps are compatible with the latest version of QBO. Outdated or incompatible app versions can lead to conflicts and failed syncing attempts.

Review Data Mapping

Data mapping defines how information is transferred between applications. Incorrect data mapping can result in mismatches between corresponding fields in different systems. Users should review data mapping settings for each integration and make adjustments as necessary.

Reauthorize Apps

Sometimes, the authorization between QBO and a third-party app may expire or become corrupted. In such cases, reauthorizing the app can reestablish the connection and resolve the syncing problem. The process usually involves logging into the third-party app and re-enabling the integration.

Contact Support

Despite thorough troubleshooting efforts, some syncing issues may persist. In such situations, reaching out to QuickBooks Online customer support is the best course of action. The support team can investigate the problem further, provide tailored guidance, and, if necessary, escalate the issue for a more in-depth resolution.

By following these comprehensive troubleshooting steps, users can overcome common issues related to connectivity and syncing in QuickBooks Online. These solutions empower users to make the most of QBO's features and ensure a seamless experience with their cloud-based accounting platform.

Tips for Improving Efficiency and Productivity in QBO

Customize Your Dashboard

The QBO dashboard serves as the central hub for users to access crucial financial information at a glance. One of the key ways to enhance efficiency in QBO is by customizing this dashboard to cater to specific business needs. By default, the dashboard displays general information such as account balances, recent transactions, and income and expense trends. However, every business is unique, and different metrics may hold more significance depending on its nature and goals.

To begin customizing the dashboard, users can add, remove, and rearrange widgets according to their preferences. Essential widgets such as cash flow trackers, bank account summaries, and accounts receivable/payable information can be placed front and center for immediate visibility. By prioritizing relevant data on the dashboard, users can save time and quickly access critical financial insights without navigating through multiple menus.

Utilize Bank Feeds

Manual data entry can be laborious, time-consuming, and susceptible to errors. To overcome this challenge, QBO offers a powerful feature known as bank feeds, which automates the process of importing financial transactions from bank and credit card accounts directly into the software. By connecting the relevant accounts, users can effortlessly sync transactions, eliminating the need for manual input.

To optimize the use of bank feeds, users should ensure that accounts are accurately linked and regularly reconcile transactions. Reconciliation involves matching the imported bank transactions with those recorded in QBO and verifying that the financial data is accurate and up-to-date. This practice not only saves time but also improves data integrity and minimizes discrepancies in financial records.

Take Advantage of Automation

Automation is a powerful ally in enhancing productivity and reducing repetitive manual tasks. QBO incorporates several automation features that can significantly streamline financial management processes. One such feature is the ability to create recurring transactions, which include invoices, bills, and expenses that occur regularly.

By setting up recurring transactions, users can specify the frequency and date for repetitive expenses or income. For instance, monthly rent, utility bills, or loan payments can be scheduled as recurring transactions, eliminating the need to recreate them each time they are due. This not only saves time but also reduces the likelihood of forgetting to enter important transactions.

Furthermore, users can automate the generation and distribution of reports with QBO's scheduled reporting feature. This allows businesses to receive essential financial reports, such as profit and loss statements or balance sheets, at predetermined intervals. Whether it's weekly, monthly, or quarterly, scheduled reports ensure that stakeholders are well-informed without manual intervention.

Another time-saving automation tool is the use of rules for categorizing transactions. QBO allows users to set up rules based on specific criteria to automatically categorize transactions. For example, transactions from a particular vendor can be automatically categorized as "office supplies." This minimizes the effort required for manual categorization and ensures consistent and accurate financial data.

Master Keyboard Shortcuts

Keyboard shortcuts are powerful tools that can significantly improve your efficiency when working with QuickBooks Online. In this chapter, we'll explore a range of keyboard shortcuts designed to streamline navigation and tasks within QuickBooks Online. These shortcuts are compatible with popular web browsers such as Internet Explorer, Firefox, and Chrome. Mac users can often substitute the CMD ⌘ key for Alt or CTRL as indicated in some shortcuts.

Accessing the Keyboard Shortcuts Reference Guide

Before delving into the shortcuts themselves, it's essential to know where to find them and how to access the Keyboard Shortcuts Reference Guide in QuickBooks Online.

- You can download and print a copy of the QuickBooks Online Keyboard Shortcuts reference guide, although it's available in English only.
- To access this guide within QuickBooks Online, simply hold Control + Option (Alt) + ? (for Mac).

Now, let's explore some valuable keyboard shortcuts within QuickBooks Online:

Opening Multiple Windows

Quickly open multiple windows to enhance your multitasking capabilities:

- For Internet Explorer: Press Ctrl + N (Note: Both windows will be signed in to the same company).
- For Firefox: Press Ctrl + N (Note: Second window won't be signed in, but you can log in to the same company for dual-screen use).
- For Chrome: Press Ctrl + N (Note: Signing in to the existing company occurs if you visit QuickBooks Online in the new window).

Text Search in a Window

Effortlessly find specific text within a window:

- Use CTRL + F (works in Internet Explorer, Firefox, and Chrome) to bring up a search pop-up window.
- Firefox opens a Find toolbar at the bottom.
- Chrome opens a search field at the top right.

Date Entry Shortcuts

Quickly input dates using these shortcuts:

- Next day: Plus key (+)
- Previous day: Minus key (-)
- Today: W
- First day of the Week: W
- Last day of the Week: K
- First day of the Month: M
- Last day of the Month: H

- First day of the Year: Y
- Last day of the Year: R
- Press Alt + down arrow to open the date pop-up calendar on a date field.

Calculation Shortcuts

Perform calculations directly within Amount or Rate fields:

- Addition: +
- Subtraction: -
- Multiplication: *
- Division: /
- Grouping: ( )

Example: 13.95 + (25.95 * 0.75)

Navigating Fields on Forms

Efficiently move between fields on most forms:

- Tab key: Forward
- Shift + Tab: Backward
- Space Bar: Check a checkbox field

Dropdown List Selection

Navigate and select items in drop-down lists:

- Press Tab until you reach the field.
- Press Alt + down arrow to open the list.
- Use up and down arrows to scroll through items.
- Press Tab to select the item and move to the next field.

Dropdown List with Sub-items

Select items in lists that contain sub-items:

- Type the first few characters of the parent item to select it.
- To access sub-items, type the first few characters of the sub-item.
- Use Alt + down arrow to open the list of sub-items.
- Navigate and select items using arrows.
- Press Tab to confirm your selection.

Saving Forms

Effortlessly save forms without using your mouse:

- From any form, press Alt + S (Alt + Shift + S for Firefox and Chrome).
- For Mac users, it's Option + Control + S.

Responding to Messages

Quickly respond to messages within QuickBooks Online:

- Hold down the Alt key. If button names are underlined, type the underlined letter while holding Alt to select the button.

Transaction Type Selection in Account Registers

Select transaction types in account registers:

- In a new, yellow transaction row, press Shift + Tab to select the transaction type field.
- Press Alt + down arrow to open the list.
- Use arrows or type the first letter of the transaction type.
- Press Tab to select and move to the next field.

Managing Ref # Field

Manipulate the Ref # field efficiently:

- + to increase the Ref #.
- - to decrease the Ref #.
- T for To Print in the Ref # field for specific transaction types.

Saving or Editing Transactions

Save or edit selected transactions swiftly:

- Save with Alt + S (Alt + Shift + S for Firefox and Chrome).
- Edit with Alt + E.

Navigating within the Register

Move seamlessly between transactions in account registers:

- Use up arrow to select the transaction above.
- Use down arrow to select the transaction below.

Adjusting Print Alignment

Fine-tune print alignment:

- Select the Vertical or Horizontal field and use + to raise the number or - to lower it. Numeric keypad keys are required.

Navigating in Journal Entries

Efficiently navigate within journal entries:

- Use up arrow to move to the distribution line above.
- Use down arrow to move to the one below.

Implement User Access Controls

As businesses grow and more individuals are involved in financial management, it becomes essential to ensure data security and integrity. QBO offers robust user access controls that allow administrators to define specific permissions for each user. By setting appropriate access levels, businesses can restrict access to sensitive financial information, ensuring that employees can only view and modify data relevant to their roles.

For instance, a bookkeeper may only need access to invoicing and expense entries, while a financial manager requires access to financial reports and cash flow data. By configuring user access controls accordingly, businesses can prevent unauthorized access to critical financial data and safeguard against potential data breaches.

Time-Saving Shortcuts and Techniques

Batch Transactions: Streamlining Repetitive Tasks

In the realm of financial management, businesses often encounter repetitive tasks involving multiple transactions. This could include sending invoices to multiple clients, entering recurring expenses, or updating sales receipts for a series of orders. Performing these actions individually can be time-consuming and prone to errors. Fortunately, QuickBooks Online (QBO) offers a powerful feature known as batch transactions, providing users with an efficient solution to handle repetitive tasks seamlessly.

Memorized Transactions: Automating Recurring Entries

Recurring transactions are a common aspect of financial management, ranging from regular monthly rent payments to subscription charges and utility bills. Manually entering the same data repeatedly can be both tedious and susceptible to human error. To address this, QuickBooks Online offers a powerful tool called memorized transactions, allowing users to automate the creation and entry of recurring transactions.

Creating memorized transactions in QBO involves the following steps:

1. Identifying Recurring Transactions: Begin by identifying the transactions that occur regularly and have consistent details. These could include monthly rent payments, loan installments, or utility bills.
2. Setting Up Memorized Transactions: Once the recurring transactions are identified, create memorized transaction templates. Enter all the necessary details, such as vendor information, amounts, and transaction dates.
3. Scheduling Memorized Transactions: QBO allows users to set up a schedule for each memorized transaction, specifying how often it should be generated. Users can choose from options like daily, weekly, monthly, or custom intervals.
4. Automatic Generation: Once the memorized transactions are set up, and the schedule is defined, QBO will automatically generate these transactions at the specified intervals. This ensures that users no longer need to manually enter recurring transactions.
5. Review and Confirmation: Regularly review the automatically generated transactions to ensure their accuracy. If there are any changes or adjustments needed, modify the memorized transaction template to reflect the updated details.

By leveraging memorized transactions, businesses can eliminate the repetitive nature of recurring entries, avoid overlooking important payments, and maintain a consistent financial record with minimal effort.

CSV Imports: Efficient Bulk Data Entry

For businesses dealing with a large volume of data, manually entering information into QuickBooks Online can be time-consuming and error-prone. To expedite the process of data entry, QBO offers the option to import data using CSV (Comma Separated Values) files. By preparing the data in a CSV format, users can efficiently update multiple records in QBO with just a few simple steps.

The process of importing data through CSV files in QBO involves the following steps:

1. **Prepare the CSV File:** Start by organizing the data into a CSV file. Each column in the CSV file should correspond to the relevant data fields in QBO. For example, if importing customer information, the columns might include name, address, email, and phone number.
2. **Map Data Fields:** After uploading the CSV file, QBO will prompt users to map the data fields in the CSV to the corresponding fields in QBO. This ensures that the data is placed in the correct locations.
3. **Verify and Confirm:** Before finalizing the import, review the mapped data to ensure accuracy. Double-check that all information is correctly placed in the appropriate fields.
4. **Import Data:** Once the data is verified, proceed with the import process. QBO will process the CSV file and update the relevant records accordingly.
5. **Review the Results:** After the import, review the updated records in QBO to confirm that all data was imported correctly. If any discrepancies are found, analyze the CSV file to identify and correct the issues before repeating the import.

By utilizing CSV imports, businesses can efficiently update large batches of data, saving significant time and reducing the risk of data entry errors.

Reports and Templates: Quick Access to Critical Information

Generating financial reports is a crucial aspect of monitoring a business's performance, but repeatedly creating the same reports can be time-consuming. QuickBooks Online offers a solution through customizable report templates, enabling users to generate essential financial reports with ease.

Creating and using report templates in QBO involves the following steps:

- **Customize Reports:** Start by customizing the reports to display the necessary financial data. Users can choose the specific metrics, date ranges, and filters that suit their reporting needs.
- **Memorize the Report:** Once the report is customized, save it as a template by memorizing it in QBO. The memorized report will retain all the specified settings and filters.
- **Accessing Memorized Reports:** To generate the report in the future, access it from the memorized report list in QBO. Users can select the appropriate template and generate the report instantly.
- **Modify Templates as Needed:** As business needs evolve, users can modify the report templates to reflect any changes. This ensures that the reports remain relevant and aligned with the business's goals.

By creating and utilizing report templates, businesses can quickly access crucial financial information, track performance metrics efficiently, and make informed decisions with up-to-date data.

Conclusion

QuickBooks Online has proven itself to be an invaluable asset in the ever-evolving landscape of business and financial management. This book has served as your steadfast companion, guiding you through the intricate realm of QBO with precision and clarity. From the foundational aspects of setting up your account to the depths of advanced features and integrations, you've journeyed through a comprehensive exploration of this powerful accounting software.

As you close this chapter of your learning journey, you're not just equipped with the technical know-how of using QuickBooks Online; you possess a profound understanding of the *why* behind each function. You grasp the significance of reconciliation, the role of the Chart of Accounts, the importance of accurate financial reporting, and so much more. This holistic comprehension ensures that you're not just a user, but a strategist using QBO to its fullest potential to drive your business's success.

Remember, your business is not just numbers and ledgers; it's a dynamic entity influenced by human factors as well. With insights into payroll and employee management, you're poised to navigate the complexities of managing your workforce while keeping your financials in check.

As you step forward, you carry with you the troubleshooting wisdom and time-saving tips that Chapter 14 has bestowed upon you. This knowledge ensures that challenges are met with solutions and opportunities are embraced with efficiency.

This book has been more than a guide; it's been your partner in deciphering the intricacies of QuickBooks Online. You've embraced its lessons, harnessed its capabilities, and now stand ready to leverage its power for your business's growth and prosperity.

With each entry, each report, and each analysis conducted within QuickBooks Online, you're charting a course toward a financially resilient future. So, whether you're a novice embarking on a new journey or a seasoned pro fine-tuning your skills, the knowledge you've gained here will be the wind in your sails as you navigate the seas of financial management.

Congratulations on completing this comprehensive guide to mastering QuickBooks Online. Your journey doesn't end here; it transforms into a dynamic voyage of strategic financial management. Welcome to the new era of empowered business operations.

Index Table